ACHIEVE MORE.

"Aimee has a way of thinking that brings new insight into what seems like every day events, but is really the essence of a modern life. Her book on bringing positive energy into living is worth a wide audience."
—Peter Block, consultant and author of *Stewardship: Choosing Service Over Self-Interest*

"This illuminating book takes a holistic approach to dealing with pressure and stress at both the individual and organizational levels. Sharing personal experiences and great stories as well as practice exercises and reflective questions, Aimee prepares us to befriend the pressures in our lives with conscious presence and skillful embodied action. I learned a lot personally and look forward to continuing the personal practices I discovered here."
—Juanita Brown, Ph.D., Co-founder, The World Café

"*Stress Less. Achieve More.* by Aimee Bernstein offers a rich blend of inspiring stories, principles, and profoundly practical skills that affirm our capacity to live and work with greater ease, strength, wisdom, vitality, and peace of mind. The world needs leaders equipped with such revolutionary wisdom!"
—Joel and Michelle Levey, Founders, Wisdom at Work, and authors of *Living in Balance: A Mindful Guide* *d*

D1005416

"There's all that other stuff out there and there is this. If I had not experienced this wise advice personally, I would not believe it. In this world of spin, it is refreshing to read such powerful and genuine words that can drive major positive change in your busy and stressful life. Aimee's holistic view is the key to the effectiveness of the approach. My only regret is that I didn't read this decades ago. . . ."

—Peter McHale, Sr. V.P. Research & Development/
Quality Control, World-class Beauty Company

"Aimee is one of a small group of new thinkers who are making themselves known to those open to ancient wisdom. She provides a map to reunite oneself with universal energy. [She] demonstrates that this reconnection can bring harmony, reduce stress, and help eliminate conflict in our lives. Her work is both progressive and practical."

—James W. Jordan, Pennsylvania Regional Director,
National Association of Mental Illness

"That 'big-heart' manifestation of Aimee's being transcends throughout this book, which will shine like a light in the darkness for many who seek psychological explanations and solutions for managing stress triggers. My personal take from her book is that the journey of change begins with the 'self,' and the better one increases awareness of one's weaknesses with an aim to improvement from mediocrity to significance, the better one will navigate the materialistic world. Ultimately, one can be a 'master of self' when one consciously and consistently submits to the greater good and with humility."

—FongTze Wong, Group Chief Corporate Communications
Officer, National Healthcare Group, Singapore

"If you are looking for a way to live and work in an energetically positive way, then *Stress Less. Achieve More.* is the book for you. It is full of ideas and practical exercises to flip your life from stressful to successful."

—Diana Whitney, Ph.D., Founder, Taos Institute, and author of *Appreciative Leadership: Focus on What Works to Drive Winning Performance and Build a Thriving Organization*

"In *Stress Less. Achieve More.*, Aimee Bernstein has provided just what the doctor should have ordered for our busy and often overwhelmed lives. This book goes beyond the standard recommendations of eating well, meditating, and getting enough sleep and looks at how to transform our underlying consciousness and body awareness. If you apply the practical actions and allow yourself to be inspired by Bernstein's stories, you will find yourself easily and gracefully standing on your leading edge."

—Judi Neal, Ph.D., Chairman and CEO, Edgewalkers International, and author of *Edgewalkers: People and Organizations That Take Risks, Build Bridges, and Break New Ground*

"Research has (surprisingly) shown that too LITTLE pressure in our lives can actually lead to poor performance. Pressure is not always a bad thing. In fact, in this well-crafted book, Aimee Bernstein teaches you how to actually maximize on pressure you may be feeling—how to turn anxiety into an ally, using time-honored techniques. Let this book completely transform how you handle pressure!"

—Brian O. Underhill, Ph.D., Executive coach and CEO, CoachSource, and author of *Executive Coaching for Results*

"Aimee Bernstein is the foremost expert on how to use pressure—the energy of change—to empower you and upgrade your performance. This book demonstrates in simple terms how to deal with stressful pressures in your professional and personal life by letting go of your resistance and opening and aligning to pressure. Become the person you've always wanted to be—more energetic, powerful, and dynamic!"
—Nancy Zentis, Ph.D., CEO, Institute for
Organization Development

STRESS LESS.
ACHIEVE MORE.

STRESS LESS. | ACHIEVE MORE.

SIMPLE WAYS TO TURN PRESSURE INTO A POSITIVE FORCE IN YOUR LIFE

Aimee Bernstein

AMACOM

AMERICAN MANAGEMENT ASSOCIATION

New York • Atlanta • Brussels • Chicago • Mexico City
San Francisco • Shanghai • Tokyo • Toronto • Washington, D.C.

Bulk discounts available. For details visit:
www.amacombooks.org/go/specialsales
Or contact special sales:
Phone: 800-250-5308
Email: specialsls@amanet.org
View all the AMACOM titles at: www.amacombooks.org
American Management Association: www.amanet.org

This publication is designed to provide accurate and authoritative information in regard to the subject matter covered. It is sold with the understanding that the publisher is not engaged in rendering legal, accounting, or other professional service. If legal advice or other expert assistance is required, the services of a competent professional person should be sought.

Library of Congress Cataloging-in-Publication Data

Bernstein, Aimee.
Stress less. Achieve more. : Simple ways to turn pressure into a positive force in your life / Aimee Bernstein.
pages cm
Includes bibliographical references and index.
ISBN 978-0-8144-3383-6 (pbk. : alk. paper)—ISBN 0-8144-3383-9 (pbk. : alk. paper)—ISBN 978-0-8144-3384-3 (ebook)
1. Stress management.   2. Self-actualization (Psychology)   I. AMACOM.   II. Title.
RA785.B4845 2014
155.9'042—dc23
2014036401

About AMA

American Management Association (www.amanet.org) is a world leader in talent development, advancing the skills of individuals to drive business success. Our mission is to support the goals of individuals and organizations through a complete range of products and services, including classroom and virtual seminars, webcasts, webinars, podcasts, conferences, corporate and government solutions, business books, and research. AMA's approach to improving performance combines experiential learning—learning through doing—with opportunities for ongoing professional growth at every step of one's career journey.

Illustrations by Raul Bonano of Crystal Clear Art

Printing number

10 9 8 7 6 5 4 3 2 1

To my beloved parents, Sally and Walter Bernstein
With deepest gratitude for your gifts of love,
kindness, and courage. Wish you were here.

To my dearest sensei and friend, Robert Nadeau
For masterfully guiding me through an energy world
that simplified and enhanced my life.

CONTENTS

Acknowledgments   xiii

Introduction: Make Friends with Pressure: Following the Clues   1

1. **Run Deeper, Not Faster:**
   Understanding Pressure from a New Perspective   9

2. **Don't Believe Everything You Think:**
   Moving Beyond the Limitations of Your Personality Type   31

3. **You Can't Get There from *Not* Here:**
   Where Is Your Attention?   55

4. **Function from Your Center:**
   Preserving Your Integrity Under Pressure   75

5. **When Things Are Bad, Envision Your Best:**
   Extending Your Energy for High Performance and Creativity   95

6. **Size Matters:**
   Becoming as Big as the Job   117

7. **Gain Control by Giving It Up:**
Resolving Conflicts Harmoniously   137

8. **Nobody Does It Alone:**
Taking Your Heart to Work   163

9. **Spark Creative Solutions in High-Pressure Situations:**
Listening Is More Than Hearing   189

Conclusion: You Reach Your Destiny in Spite of Yourself   215

Resources   225

Notes   229

Index   233

About the Author   241

ACKNOWLEDGMENTS

To Stephen Samuels for the countless hours of instruction in meditative practices, the informative and at times life-changing conversations, and the decades of friendship.

To my agent, Michael Snell, for believing in me and this project through all the curves in the road.

To Ellen Kadin of AMACOM for choosing to publish this book and for being in my corner every step of the way.

To my development editor, Ellen Coleman, for your willingness to remain open-minded while discussing different points of view, for your extraordinary editing ability, and for confronting me with questions like *what is energy*.

To AMACOM associate editor, Erika Spelman, for your kind guidance and expertise.

To Martine Marie for the fabulous suggestions that made this book better and for being such an extraordinary support and friend.

To Diana Daffner, Jim Jordan, Chris Thorsen, Richard Moon, Donna Garske, Dinesh Chandra, and the folks at the Broward Zen Center (Carole, Mark, Philip, Walter . . .) for the hours of conversation that helped me clarify my thinking.

To Lance Belew of LookN2IT for creating a website for *Stress Less. Achieve More.* that shines as bright as your friendship and your songs.

To Ted Potter of Tech Marin for the patient and kind way you solve my tech dilemmas.

To Dennis Nadeau of Card Genius for the videos, the great advice, and for always being willing to help. You are a class act!

To Marcella Brekken and Milkweed Editions for allowing me to use Bill Holm's wonderful poem "Advice."

To Veta Gayle for taking such good care of my mother that I had time and peace of mind to write this book.

To all the people who generously shared their stories in this book.

And to my best friend, Felicia (Felice) Horner, who for decades has been there to celebrate my highs and provide me with a soft place to land when I am low.

Thank you all.

MAKE FRIENDS WITH PRESSURE

Following the Clues

The next message you need is always right where you are.

—Ram Dass, American spiritual leader and author

t's Humanitarian Day at the United Nations. As the seats in the General Assembly fill up, the excitement is palpable. Onto the stage steps Beyoncé, dressed in an elegant long white sequined dress. With the symbol of the United Nations behind her, she stops center stage and waits for the music to begin. The pressure must be enormous, yet she is so centered and upright, she doesn't display it. She begins to sing "I Was Here," a song that encourages people to use their lives for the common good. Behind her, a video shows people from around the world. For a moment her hand rests on her heart. The camera immediately pans to members of the audience, who are clearly touched by her presence and words.

The music builds; her energy intensifies, embracing the far reaches of the hall. Her arm naturally rises to align with her center and then sweeps across her body in a semicircle. Behind her, a video of rescue efforts plays; the emotion builds, then the audience rises. Beyoncé arches her back, lifting her arms, chest, and head as if empowered by a force from above. She bends her knees, and as she straightens, I can see that she is deeply grounded. Her voice becomes more compelling as her body movements emphasize her words. When she is done, she stands erect, fully present and quiet, seemingly undisturbed by the magnitude of energy that has just pulsated through her. I watch this video countless times, each time spotting the clues to how she befriends pressure, which might otherwise create stress, and I know that I have witnessed a master.

Although few of us achieve such proficiency, life provides us with clues to teach us how to use pressure by pointing the way to an ideal state in which our mind/body/energy system is open and aligned with the larger energy field that nurtures and sustains us. No one, even scientists, knows exactly what energy is; however, for our purposes I define it as an electromagnetic vibration that composes and connects all life by transmitting information. We can't always perceive energy, but it is always there, and when the personal and universal energy fields unite, the feeling is extraordinary—inspiring, empowering, confidence-building, and peaceful. In these moments the energy that was pressing on us becomes the fuel that uplifts, making us feel as big as the challenges we face. As our decisions and actions reflect our inner state, we lead and function more effectively and effortlessly. Not only do we cognitively understand the essence of leadership, we embody it.

To live more consistently in this ideal state, and lead a "stress less" life, we need to identify and sense/feel the clues and the changes we need to make. That's what this book is about. Much of the time, however, we are so engrossed in our life dramas—I was promoted; my boss micromanages me; I didn't get the account—that we fail to ask the bigger questions and thus miss the clues. Yet, if you step back and review your experiences with the detached eye of a researcher, you would notice certain energetic habits—repetitive tendencies—that run through your stories. These repetitive tendencies are the ways you typically interact with energy. For example, you may discover that your fear of being swallowed up by your team's expectations really results from a frequent lack of energy coming from you (outflow), which limits your ability to participate and express yourself fully. Similarly, your frustration with your boss's autocratic style might stem from an inability to stand rooted in your own power (as Beyoncé did). If you could, you would not feel victimized by the boss's need to control.

Energetic habits underline and inform all of our perceptual, emotional, and behavioral patterns. Change these habits and it is easier and faster to break free from limiting self-definitions, emotional reactions, and behaviors. Similarly, by paying attention to when you are high performing, confident, and happy, you will begin to spot the energetic habits that align you with the larger energy field. Noticing what works provides a process that transforms pressure from an enemy into an ally and makes what is extraordinary seem ordinary.

HOW THIS BOOK WILL EMPOWER YOU

Stress Less. Achieve More. offers a step-by-step map with practical exercises for you and your team to turn pressure into a positive force. Instead of focusing solely on diminishing the pressure in your busy life, which may be unrealistic, I'll show you how to expand your capacity for handling increased amounts of pressure while rediscovering the wonder of being alive. As an executive coach, psychotherapist, trainer, and organizational consultant, I have used this process with hundreds of clients including senior and mid-level managers of Fortune 500 companies, psychologists, professionals, scientists, and artists with extraordinary results. By shifting their energetic patterns, they learned to effortlessly transform their limited reactive habits and function more skillfully. In most cases, they reported an expanded sense of self not dominated by their egos, a heightened sense of connection, and an increased ease and effectiveness in handling professional and personal challenges.

As you will read, I didn't come to this knowledge without help. Instead, I was blessed to find an extraordinary teacher, Robert Nadeau, a seventh dan aikido master and inner researcher of states of consciousness, whose work has been the subject of numerous books. Today, the work of scientists validates the things he taught over thirty years ago.

Even before I met Bob, I collected clues about how to relate effectively to pressure, although I didn't yet understand them or their significance. I offer you my story with the hope that it inspires you to review the clues in your life and encourages you to make time to think about when you were at your best under pressure. What was unusual about this experience? What did you feel and sense at the time? What did you learn from your experience? You may discover that you know more than you think about using pressure to your advantage without hurting yourself or others.

COLLECT CLUES: DISCOVER WHAT WORKS FOR YOU

When I was seven, I experienced my first *petit mal* seizure, a mild form of epilepsy. Though I outgrew it by age thirteen, the memory of the seizures and the symptoms leading up to them remains fresh. Physical exertion and/or emotional stress triggered an attack. During these times, I felt my consciousness lift upwards through my body. My legs became weak, and I lost all sense of connection with the ground. Simultaneously, my world contracted and darkened; it was as if the space around me was being sucked into a vortex over which I had no control. Out of the silence, I heard a sound similar to an ocean's whooshing resonate in my ears. Then I lost consciousness.

I now know these episodes resulted from my inability to handle pressure. My attention was habitually located outside myself in others; I was more aware of what they thought, felt, and sensed than what I did. I easily took in other people's pain and tension without consciously realizing it. To survive I became a helper and a fixer.

Fortunately, my parents recognized I had a talent for dance and sent me to dance school. My teacher's name was Marjorie Marshall. Today she is probably best known as the mother of movie directors Penny and

Gary Marshall, but to me she stands out as the first person to show me how to use pressure positively. Her school was located in the basement of a Bronx apartment building, but entering it was magical. Here the pressure of sound, physical exertion, and my teacher's demands were fuel that expanded rather than diminished me. As I let go of my self-consciousness and need to understand, please, and control, I felt centered and grounded in my body. This inner balance gave me a sense of extraordinary well-being. As I followed the pulsations that arose from my deepest core, I was transformed from a physical body in motion into a boundless energy field. I felt released and connected to something much larger than myself. I was present and fully myself. I was free.

The ability to handle pressure might have eluded me had it not been for Marjorie Marshall. She was the first person (other than my parents) to teach me discipline and its importance in coping during difficult times. Influenced by the precision dancing of the Radio City Rockettes, Marjorie made us practice our tap dance routines until we were all perfectly in step and in line. We had to be aware of our bodies' physical boundaries as well as the space between us. Though I didn't realize it, we were developing our kinesthetic sense by learning to shift our attention from our thoughts *into* our bodies and energy fields, which prevented us from bumping into one another. Note I said into, *not* onto, our bodies: That's because you can't sense/feel unless your attention is focused inside your body, *not* on it.

Despite this training, I still didn't know how to translate what I had learned from dancing to other areas of my life. In fact, it never dawned on me that this was possible. Nor did I know how to intentionally call up the larger me that occasionally appeared while dancing. A year after joining the school, my mother went to work and my dancing career ended. I now realize that dance provided me with a large experiential clue to handling the pressures of life. Fifteen years later, life provided me with the next level of my education.

THE INNER MAP TO "STRESSLESSNESS"

In 1978, I began studying aikido with Robert Nadeau. Unlike many martial arts teachers, his focus is more on functioning better in the world than it is on learning the techniques. Training put us under pressure: not just the pressure of another's attack, which was a metaphor for life's challenges, but also the pressure that came from our own systems, which rose up in response to the attack. Instead of being eaten up by pressure, we learned through practice to open up and allow it to stream through our mind/body/energy systems. As we surrendered to the experience, we found ourselves connected to a higher level of consciousness that enhanced our perceptions and performance.

To aid us, Bob offered a simple inner map that focused on attention, center, ground, and energy, or "ki" outflow. Together these elements, when in a large enough space, birth a new identity that is more creative and capable of handling pressure. Think of it as you would a plant that, when fed the right nutrients and placed in a bigger pot, grows taller and stronger because it has the room to grow deeper roots. As we practiced each of these skills individually and together within aikido techniques, new pathways became imprinted on our nervous systems, enabling us to bypass our habitual modes of reacting and shift to a more responsive and effective way of being and behaving.

These elements actually operate as a whole, but to help you understand them better, I discuss them in separate chapters after first laying the foundation for why this map is so important for high performance and quality of life. Thus, Chapter 1 sets the context for the book. In it I discuss the accelerated pressure most people experience in the workplace, the essence of pressure and how it differs from stress, and why the usual approaches to stress reduction are not enough in today's fast-paced world. It concludes with a formula for mastery under pressure.

Chapter 2 focuses on the mental patterns that arise from our personality type and how these affect our perceptions and actions under pressure. This information is based on the Enneagram, an ancient Sufi tool that describes nine personality types. As more organizations recognize the influence of personality on work relationships, decisions, and actions, the Enneagram is quickly gaining prominence. In this chapter as well as Chapters 6 and 7 you'll find information about your personality's coping style and stress triggers. The internal energy map is the focus of Chapters 3 through 6. These chapters offer an in-depth view of habits of attention that center, ground, and extend your intrinsic energy and spaciousness. In these chapters I also discuss why these components are essential to using pressure wisely, as well as how each of them translates to the workplace.

With the map serving as our guide, Chapter 7 focuses on resolving conflict harmoniously (the essence of aikido), while Chapter 8 addresses moving through pressure by connecting with your heart, not your mind. In Chapter 9 we look at sparking creative solutions to high-pressure situations by listening to our inner wisdom. I conclude by bringing us full circle and focusing on issues of faith, hope, destiny, and the importance of clues in dealing with *all* our experiences of pressure.

Although no book can replace the clarity and power a skilled teacher brings to learning, I have designed the book as a guide to start you on your way. Throughout you'll see quotations that I call "seeds of truth," which highlight key points and, I hope, make the ideas memorable. Sections called Personal Practice contain mind/body/energy practices and reflective questions to spark new ideas and levels of understanding. Finally, each chapter contains a section titled Application for Teams to help you reduce stress in your team and/or workplace and encourage collaboration and high performance.

For more advanced readers who are already involved in meditation and/or other spiritual practices, *Stress Less. Achieve More.* will increase your ability to work with pressure throughout your daily life and deepen your current practices. Please use this book however you choose. Whether or not you do the exercises or read the book fully, you will find that particular something that you need to know now. There is no right or wrong. For those who are deeply attracted to this work and would like to participate in a training program, you'll find my contact information in the back of the book as well as the names and contact information of practitioners doing similar work.

In looking back at the mosaic of clues I have been given and the teachers who have guided my way, I see how perfectly my life has unfolded. What began as a search for understanding over thirty-five years ago quickly moved beyond the realm of curiosity and cognitive knowledge to incorporate an experiential knowing. I am blessed to have learned an easy, effective, and joyful way to enhance my performance and the quality of my life. This book represents my opportunity to share what I've learned.

ONE

RUN DEEPER, NOT FASTER

Understanding Pressure from a New Perspective

Progress might have been all right once, but it has gone on too long.

—Ogden Nash

"I'm buried in work," bemoans my friend Ben, an attorney specializing in elderly issues.

"I'm glad you're making money," I say. "Living in Marin County, California, with a wife and two preteen daughters, you had better be bringing in the big bucks," I tease.

"Yeah, I'm doing okay," he halfheartedly agrees. A long pause ensues.

"Are you?" I ask gently. "Many people in business tell me that they're buried in their work. That's scary. 'Buried' is such a negative image, an inability to breathe, compression, and contraction. And the images 'stretched thin' conjures up aren't pretty either."

Ben says nothing. He's come a long way from the twenty-one-year-old I met decades ago when he eked out a living as a freelance researcher. In those days, he wouldn't think twice about taking a walk in the woods during the day instead of staying glued to his desk. Finally, he declares, "I love my work," pauses again, then says, "I just wish it wasn't so relentless."

That's the rub for many of us. According to statistics only 25 percent of us love our work, but even if we are among the fortunate who do, the constant pressures wear us down. We are besieged by information with the expectation that we are available 24/7 and know the right answer the moment we are called on to make a decision. The unspoken assumption is that we will handle constant demands and interruptions with ease while being psychologically astute enough to coach the smiling, backstabbing employee who wants our job or the associate having an emotional meltdown in our office. When we don't rise to these expectations, we feel bad about ourselves or angry.

In addition, instead of technology making our lives easier and giving us more free time, many of us become addicted to it, spending countless hours not only at work but at home on email, social media, and our smartphones. Furthermore, we know we need to spend more time with our families or carve out time for a social life, yet, as Ben said, "it's all so relentless" that it's hard to find the time.

At work, many of the jobs we want to do get pushed to the back burner while the have-to-dos continually tug at us. So we run faster and rely too often on our willpower and force to get through the day, which exhausts us. In the process, the joy of work often dissipates, as does our deep connection with ourselves. Perhaps when we dream of a higher quality of life, we tell ourselves to be grateful that we have a job, and, of course, that's true. But what a cost we pay!

As Scott Barrett, a successful and now balanced leader, relates:

"I had the opportunity to climb the ladder and get very high. When I was in my mid-thirties, I was the president of a billion dollar company with 50,000 employees. When I got to the top of the ladder, I realized I had pretty much destroyed my family, my relationship with my wife, and didn't really have a relationship with my faith. I asked myself, *where do I go from here? What did I gain?* We all get that wake-up call. It's a matter of whether we are going to listen to it. For me, the knock had to be pretty loud."

If we choose to listen, the body provides plenty of clues. Under continuous demands and pressure, the thinking mind works overtime. After a while, it becomes less efficient and harder to turn off. Sleep patterns may become disturbed; worry, doubts, and fears may arise; and depression or violent behavior may emerge. In its debilitated state, the body breaks down and disease occurs. However, it doesn't have to be this way. Later in his career, Scott became the chief information officer for a large public firm. His experience working with Wayne Huizenga, then chairman and chief executive of the company, birthed these observations:

"It doesn't matter if you are the CEO of the company or a programmer. How you handle pressure and the activity going on around you matters. I learned a lot about handling pressure from Wayne. He could be there before everybody started in the morning and after everybody left. He went from meeting to meeting dealing with a broad range of issues. The pace was rapid, yet it neither restricted nor bothered him. There was never any friction. He just dealt with each issue that came up and was pleasant to be with all the time; his demeanor never changed. And a tremendous amount got done.

"Later, another man took over the presidency. He worked just as long and as hard as Wayne; meetings still started at 5:00 or 6:00 AM. Over time, the job took its toll on him physically and emotionally. Did you ever see the before and after pictures of U.S. presidents? It was like that. He came in looking okay but six months later, he looked like death warmed over. All the activity, the pace, and the pressure were dragging on him. It wasn't frictionless. His dealings with people suffered as well because he was worn down."

Each of us has a habitual way of responding when the pressure builds. Some of us lose our strength and collapse while others resist and harden. Then there are those who either have a natural ability to be strong under pressure or have learned this skill. Without knowing it, they reconfigure their brains to avoid being flooded by cortisol, the stress hormone. Now that's a very good thing since cortisol can shrink brain mass, take ten years off your life, and negatively affect your organs, not to mention your ability to get along with others. Those who are very skilled at handling stressors can even trigger the release of serotonin, the well-being hormone, and that attitude can be transmitted to others by what you say and do. However, for those who have little skill in transforming pressure into a positive force, it not only negatively affects them, it can affect those around them. To begin to change these patterns, we need to understand pressure from a new perspective.

PRESSURE IN THE TWENTY-FIRST CENTURY

Although some call this century the Information Age, I believe at its core, it is the Energy Age. Just as the Internet and satellite systems have changed the nature of information exchange, lasers, acupuncture, and ultrasound as well as apps that read such things as high blood pressure[1] and the electrical activity of the heart are transforming medicine. Quantum physicists recognize that humans are energy beings living in a sea of energy. They acknowledge that solid objects are composed of both particles and waves. Biologists recognize the telepathic communication of animals, and psychologists have validated the ability of humans to intuit and communicate in this way. Furthermore, there is a growing understanding that certain places and people have a negative effect on the immune system while others seem to support well-being. Increasingly, scientists recognize that to understand ourselves, simply studying physical structure is often not enough; we must also study the patterns and flows of our intrinsic energy, which give rise to the physical structure. For this reason in our discussion of how to use pressure as a positive force, we will examine the physical, emotional, behavioral, and energetic aspects of who we are. For now, let's begin by defining pressure.

Pressure Redefined

Imagine that in five minutes you will present a speech to thousands of people. In the audience are your boss, colleagues, family members, love interests, and everyone you would like to impress but may not even know. As you pretend, pay attention to your thoughts and what is going on in your body. Now let's imagine that in thirty seconds you will take your place on the stage and the curtain will rise. From behind the curtain, you spot President Obama and the First Lady walking into the hall. Can you feel the rush? How would you describe what is going on now in your mind and body? Are you comfortable in your skin or would you rather be fishing?

Whether or not you like performing, being on stage usually calls up a great deal of energy. Common effects include sweaty palms, racing heart, wobbly legs, the inability to catch your breath, and an adrenalin rush that does not feel like it can be controlled or contained. More profound life experiences such as war, birth, the death of a loved one, and natural and unnatural disasters turn the barometer up exponentially. These experiences are so powerful that they sometimes shatter us.

Extreme experiences are not the only ones that call up energy; everyday occurrences may also push us off balance. Think about the promotion that didn't come, the stack of unpaid bills, or the dates who said you were nice but not their type. Then again, think about the excitement you felt when the new client chose you, not your competitor; your first hot sports car; or the sudden realization that your creative idea is not only good, it rocks. It makes no difference whether these situations were good or bad, whether they were planned or sudden, acute or chronic, internally or externally driven. Each of them calls up energy through your mind/body/energy field. Some are big rushes, some are smaller flows, and some you may not even notice. Some may feel good and some may not. Nevertheless, in each experience, you are dancing with the pressure of life.

According to Webster's dictionary, pressure is the "exertion of force (strength, energy, power) upon a surface by an object, fluid, etc. in contact with it." Words, feelings, actions, situations, and environments contain energy or power that "exert a force" upon our mind/body system. Usually we think about pressure negatively as a weighted sense of concentrated energy that is *pushing* on us. "I want to see you in my office," your boss says and, even if you have done nothing wrong, you just may notice your muscles tighten. Walk into a room where people are stressed and you'll probably start feeling tense. Isolate yourself, and you still may feel the pressure created by your own thoughts or perhaps by a slight imbalance you can't even name. We are constantly being affected by the energies we come in contact with whether we are aware of them or not.

Although we may seek pressureless environments to relax in or ways to distract ourselves from pressure, without pressure we may not have any drive or direction. Pressure then can be a very good thing. As exemplified by the earlier observation of Wayne Huizenga, sometimes pressure is a concentrated force of energy that *propels* us and generates high performance, keener perceptions, and an enhanced quality of life. It all depends on how we relate to it. Furthermore, one person's pressure is another's pleasure and vice versa. "I love cold calling," a sales manager told me. "I love the hunt, the seduction, the win." "It's the least favorite part of my job," another confessed. "I like to build relationships and build my business on word of mouth." Pressure then is our personal experience of concentrated energy encountering our mind/body system.

High performance under pressure begins with celebrating pressure as the energy of life and the energy of change. When we ease away from the habit of trying to master life by controlling or resisting it, we transform pressure from an enemy into an ally. Instead of being our number one excuse for bad behavior, pressure empowers us to become the next best version of who we really are.

IT'S NOT THE PRESSURE, IT'S HOW YOU RELATE TO IT

Whenever we are faced with a task, energy in the amount equal to the job immediately streams through our mind/body system to help us accomplish it. If we align with and are open to this flow of energy, we experience a power and aliveness that allow us to accomplish our task efficiently and effectively. At these times, we become energized by our work. Some call this "being in the zone." When we do not line up with this flow or when we resist it, we experience stress and are less able to perform. We may say then that the flow of life is like a river; the individual is a swimmer in it. When we swim with the current, it helps us; when we turn against the current, we feel stressed. What matters is not whether we are under pressure—we always are. It is how much pressure we are under and how we relate to it that matters.

The Conventional Approach to Handling Pressure

For those people ready to change their limited approach to pressure, modern medicine extols the virtues of diet, exercise, and meditation for reducing stress. If you've tried these approaches, you know they work. However, given our hectic schedules and the high-pressure world we live in, do they work well enough? The simple answer is NO.

First, they require us to take time away from work to practice them. For most of us, that's unrealistic. We're just too busy and most workplaces unfortunately still consider time away from the action as unproductive.

Second, the state of consciousness required for relaxation does not always transfer well to other activities or situations in our lives. For most of us, it's too easy for the well-being we find in the yoga class to dissipate in the face of highway gridlock, and too easy for the balance and strength we discover in the gym to evaporate the moment we are taken to task by our boss. Why is that?

Stress reduction methods imprint a new neural pathway on the nervous system, but when you are under a great deal of pressure, it is likely to trigger your old reactive pattern. As it is a more deeply imprinted pattern, it is stronger than your newer response.

Furthermore, states of consciousness depend on the body and brain's level of arousal, which changes constantly throughout the day. When we are fearful or excited, the brain processes information more quickly and our heart rate, sweat levels, and other autonomic activities speed up. When we relax, these rates slow. How we store and later retrieve memories is connected to these arousal levels. Therefore, we remember events best when we are in the same arousal state as when we experienced them. This makes the deep relaxation we experience in meditation, for example, challenging to access while in our everyday state of consciousness and even harder when we are very upset. It is as if a level of amnesia exists between one state of arousal and another.[2]

The Twenty-First Century Approach to Handling Pressure

However, imagine what you could accomplish if you were able to access different states of consciousness at will. Jim Dixon, a former Vietnam helicopter pilot and president of such companies as Nextel, Cellular One, and McCaw's Southeast Region, as well as a student of aikido, shared his experience:

> "Years ago, we tested our telecommunications system for the first time with a group of financial analysts from all over the country. Given the publicity that would ensue, it was a high-risk move. And our team really felt the pressure because we had experienced a series of setbacks and last-minute efforts to bring about this

demonstration conference call. We were in the middle of the conference call when the call dropped. It was my worst fear come true.

"While the technical team tried to reestablish the call, I felt immense pressure; it was as if I was facing an attacker. I quickly composed myself by simply reverting to my aikido training. My body remembered how to dissipate the energy, how to continue breathing deeply, and how to stay focused on the task at hand.

"The call was connected, and it proceeded extremely well. Afterward, we received excellent technical marks and, surprisingly, high praise for how well the management team handled the crisis: 'They seemed unflappable . . . they didn't even blink in the face of potential disaster.'

"In that moment, I had to be highly effective in the midst of chaos, and something automatically kicked in. Not a mental process; frankly, the words would have taken too long. I didn't consciously order myself to do it, but I let myself do it by allowing the patterns imprinted in my nervous system through the aikido practices to take over. It was similar to being in command in a combat situation. There are moments when you just have to have it together. I am sure the very basic aikido practices trigger a natural ability that is within us all."

LEADERSHIP UNDER PRESSURE

Think about the leaders you most admire. Most likely, it's not their authority, title, or even their intellect that makes you want to follow them. Instead, it's their authenticity and ability to be masters of themselves even under the most turbulent conditions. Such leaders are not egocentric but choose to serve the greater good. Instead of being unmovable in their positions, they can take a stance while still maintaining an open-minded, spacious presence. These extraordinary leaders are focused, emotionally intelligent, decisive, and skillful in action. They inspire trust, engage, and uplift people because who they are, what they say, and how they behave are consistent. They don't just talk about leadership; they embody it, even under pressure.

Mastering Leadership Under Pressure

Embodied leaders make these leadership qualities concrete. They become second nature, like a dancer's surefootedness or a great athlete's ability to swing the bat. As Dixon's experience demonstrates, this allows you to bypass thoughts and emotions that can paralyze, weaken, or cause you to lash out inappropriately. It keeps your focus on what is important and opens you up to new choices and creative solutions. When you perceive experiences from an embodied point of view, sensory feedback is immediate, and intuition or gut feelings are heightened.

THE FIRST ESSENTIAL ELEMENT: AWARENESS

The first essential element for mastery is awareness. As the self-observer in us develops, we are better able to assess our inner resources and motivations and become alert to nuances and relationships among our experiences that we hadn't previously noticed. In doing so, we are better able to compare our actions, including our habits, with our values and ideals. Thus, the first step in breaking free of habits that limit us is to identify our patterns, be they mental, emotional, behavioral, or energetic.

Insights, though delicious to chew on, do not necessitate change. Even when they generate new behavior, we often lack the energy to sustain the change. Just think of your New Year's resolutions. For awareness to be most effective, your mind needs to partner with your body—the place of emotions, sensations, and actions.

THE SECOND ESSENTIAL ELEMENT: HERENESS

I call the ability to show up and be present in the body "hereness," which is the second essential element. Here's an example of what I mean: A number of years ago, I was hired to help an information technology team improve communication and teamwork. One particular meeting with this team stands out. I was facilitating a discussion between the three men and two women about what was preventing their department from becoming a learning organization. The meeting went on for thirty minutes, and it was clear they'd had the same conversation and made the same excuses many times: "Too much to do and not enough hands to do it . . . We don't have time to learn . . . We are under too much pressure and have too many projects . . . Corporate doesn't understand our situation and doesn't take our needs into consideration . . ."

Larry, a team member, disagreed. He said everything was fine; they were not victims. The others agreed that they were not victims, but reiterated that there was too much work. They were stuck in blame, the self-defensive game.

Larry, having said his piece, had clearly disassociated himself from the conversation and was now sitting with his arms folded over his chest, leaning back in his chair. Similarly, Gene, the "I don't say much unless it's really important" guy, seemed to have shrunk into himself. The rest of the members continued the correct "corporate babble." Only Marcia, the team's leader, seemed to be alive and present. Occasionally, she voiced her frustrations, her vision of what was possible, and prodded others to come up with solutions. But there was little true dialogue and even less passion. Yet I knew these people cared about their work and each other. They were bright, well meaning, and very good at what they did.

How could it be that there were five people sitting at a conference table and all but one was not really there, and she was present only some of the time? In an attempt to jolt them into the moment, with my tongue firmly in my cheek, I told them of a new corporate policy that was sweeping across America: Only a person's head may attend meetings; their bodies, hearts, and spirits must stay home. At first, they seemed to take no notice; they were really not present. I continued the tale, making it more elaborate and fantastical as I went. Eventually, faint smiles, and finally, a real breakthrough. Gene, who seemed to have visualized this image and found it amusing, sat up straight, took a breath, and smiled broadly. He appeared more alert, more present. At last, he spoke about his real feelings regarding the workload and his desire to grow. The others perked up as he spoke, and a deeper, more authentic conversation began.

To get to this place, you must shift your attention from your thinking mind—the place where you observe and evaluate action—to your mind/ body where action occurs. Awareness of your body's sensations, feelings, moods, and movements provides experiential information about how you are in the moment. As you fine-tune your internal listening and relax, your body naturally shifts to reflect that feeling. In fact, if you think about what you are doing, you tend to stumble or lose your flow.

I'm on the mat with my aikido teacher, Robert Nadeau. He attacks with a strike to the head. I counter and he falls. For an instant, while still holding his wrist, I shift my attention to check the results. Nadeau senses the opening, and . . . boom! . . . I am sprawled on the mat. "Did you get it?" he asks.

Musicians, dancers, and athletes are obvious exemplars of those who have physically learned and epitomize the knowledge and skills of their trade. However, in every profession, the best of the best have done the same. Practice imprints the new behavior on the nervous system. It does it so well that, research suggests, within thirty days you can call it up when you need it. Continued practice allows you to do it under increasing levels of pressure. Focusing your attention on your mind/body also increases your power of intuition and provides an internal "truth-o-meter," so you can more easily sense when your decisions or the situations you find yourself in do not ring true.

If you are able to show up fully in certain situations but lack the awareness of how you became present, your extraordinary performance will be a random occurrence. Furthermore, without self-awareness, you won't be able to translate your knowledge to other aspects of your life. I am reminded of a Grammy-winning piano player who, while at the piano, was so centered and grounded that inspiration and creativity

A Seed of Truth

"Learning is experience.
All the rest is just information."
—ALBERT EINSTEIN

poured through him. Away from the piano, he was needy, insecure, and lacked integrity, which showed up in his behavior. Without awareness of what made him so masterful at the piano and able to handle the pressures of performing, he floundered miserably in his life.

THE THIRD ESSENTIAL ELEMENT: SKILLFUL ACTION

Skillful action is an activity that produces results intrinsic to your success: in this case, your business success.

As Richard Strozzi-Heckler of the Strozzi Institute, an organization that offers training in embodied leadership, shared:

> "You can sit very still and be in action. You can be running around engaging in one activity after another and there may be no action at all. The intent of action is to take care of something larger than simply performing a task. For example, if I need a ditch to put plumbing in, the people digging the ditch may not be in action, as they may not be connected to the reason for the ditch. However, the person who has the vision of better plumbing for better water usage, better toilet facilities, better water conservation, etc., may not be performing the action of digging, but is in action because that person has the intent and vision."

Skillful action arises from a clear mind/body intention. Since it arises from a connection with something larger than your ego, it provides a discernment that helps you choose between the many opportunities that

A Seed of Truth

"The journey begins right here. In the middle of the road, right beneath your feet. This is the place. There is no other place, and no other time."
—DAVID WHYTE

life presents. Skillful action is impeccable because it increases your energy rather than tiring you. Skillful action is the manifestation of a harmonious relationship to pressure.

Once you learn to embody the basic elements of the map described in the Introduction, you will be able to translate it to any activity, situation, or relationship in your life. Thus, for example, instead of having to learn how to handle the pressures of public speaking, asking for a raise, or walking down a blind alley at night—three distinctly different experiences—you will have an internal map or template to guide you in moving skillfully through each of them.

Of course, that does not mean that you will never go ballistic or have a pity party again. Being human provides many opportunities to ride the emotional edge. In my experience, practicing the simple energy awareness exercises described in each chapter continues to create a new improved normal in my ability to respond when under pressure. Like a skilled musician who makes a mistake, I have learned (and am still learning) how to move quickly from the "oops" to regain my composure. With the understanding that we are all works in progress, here is the formula for mastery under pressure:

Awareness + Hereness = Skillful Action

The hidden gift of these high-pressure times is that they force you to confront the question, *Am I running deeper or just faster?* They compel us to take a clear look at how we define ourselves, what we value, the choices we make, the skillfulness of our actions, and how we keep ourselves stuck in familiar patterns that no longer serve us well. In good times or in bad, pressure offers the power to turbocharge and transform us into the next best version of who we are. Are you ready for the ride?

PERSONAL PRACTICE

ASSESSING YOUR CURRENT APPROACH
TO PRESSURE MANAGEMENT

Think of a recent situation when you were under pressure. It may have been when you asked your boss for a raise, had a deadline to meet, or when you were in a conflict with a loved one or a colleague. What did you do to handle the pressure you felt? How well did your methods work for you? In the first column, list the three stress reduction approaches you use most often. In the second column list the benefits of the method, and in the third column list its limitations.

APPROACH	BENEFITS	LIMITATIONS

What effects do your stress reduction approaches have on your overall performance and well-being? Are you satisfied with the results? If not, perhaps it's time to try something new.

IIII▶ PRACTICE: BREATHING

In every wisdom tradition, breath is the first tool for optimal health and the reduction of stress. Yet, if you were tracking it, you would be amazed at how often you hold your breath or breathe very shallowly. Check it out now. Where in your body does your breath begin and where does it move? If you are like most people, your breath rises in the chest and the rib cage moves up. If that's the case, you're breathing enough to keep you alive, but not enough to effectively dance with the pressures of life. Without knowing it, you've energetically cut off the bottom half of your body— your belly and your legs—thereby limiting your power. Now try this:

1. Either sitting in a chair or lying down, with your knees up to support your back, put one hand approximately four inches below your belly button, which is your center of gravity, and the other hand on your lower back.

2. Now take a big breath through your nose and allow the whole area around your belly, hips, and lower back to expand. It may feel like a balloon that is being filled with air.

3. Allow the breath to expand your rib cage so your ribs are moving wide instead of up.

4. Allow the breath to continue to move up, expanding your chest and flowing into your neck and head.

5. Let it wash down your back, and exhale through your mouth. If you are comfortable with this, make an "AH" sound, which will relax you

even more. The exhale is the part of the breath cycle that relaxes you and rids your body of carbon dioxide, so let it be longer than the inhale.

6. While exhaling, notice your belly moving towards your spine. Breathe slowly, listening to your body's urge to breathe to find your unique rhythm. As you practice, notice whether you can sense the breath settling down your legs, feet, and into the ground as you exhale. Feels good, doesn't it?

Even with practice, at times you may become so immersed in your activities or situations that you forget to breathe. Here are a couple of rituals to help you remember:

- Before getting out of bed in the morning, take a couple of deep breaths. Do the same at night to help you de-stress.
- Put a Post-it with the word BREATHE on your computer monitor. Whenever you sit down at your computer or before you write the next email, take a deep cleansing breath.
- Try to catch yourself if you hold your breath or breathe shallowly. Does being with certain people or in specific situations trigger this? Are you holding yourself back from speaking your truth? If so, choose one situation and practice deep breathing before entering it, while you are in it, and after you leave.

APPLICATION FOR TEAMS

ASSESS YOUR TEAM'S PERFORMANCE UNDER PRESSURE

Some teams perform well under the everyday pressures of the workplace but choke in crises. Other teams excel when the pressure is high but seem to fizzle in the everyday. Still others perform well in both the everyday and in turbulent times, yet the price they pay in terms of stress is too high. Then there are those rare champion teams who make high performance under any condition look effortless. Which type of team do you lead?

To begin to build your dream team, you'll need to assess which aspects of your organizational systems, processes, and culture support excellence and which diminish it, particularly when under pressure. Here are some questions that might help. Use those that resonate for you and your team.

- Under what conditions do you perform and feel at your best?
- Think about a high-pressure situation in which your team produced extraordinary results without taking a toll on individual members or the team. What elements came together to generate it?
- What processes or systems add stress to the workplace; which bring ease? What about them produces this result? Do they support high performance or diminish it?
- What cultural mores add stress; which bring ease? What is it about them that produce this result? Do they support high performance or diminish it?
- What are the three top stressors in your work environment? Prioritize these. How would you change the first one? If you cannot eliminate it (e.g., constant demands or changes made by the CEO), what is under your influence or control that can take some of the pressure off?
- In terms of the workplace, what keeps you up at night?
- If you had free rein and no possible way of failing, what one change would you make to your workplace that would increase your performance under pressure and enhance the quality of your work life? Why is this one so important to you?

To get the most honest and complete answers from your team to these questions, you'll need to choose the format you'll use to generate this feedback. If you have the money, consider hiring an external consul-tant to individually interview team members or facilitate small group feedback sessions. If your division is too large, ask departments to se-lect the participants. Neutral outsiders provide confidentiality, are non-political, and can probe because they don't have an agenda.

If you don't have the budget for or interest in hiring a professional dialogue facilitator, consider how you can gather feedback on team as-sessment questions such as those posed earlier. Is there a respected person in your organization who helps to design and execute key meet-ings? Or is there someone who has shown a special talent for working with groups?

Since there is an unspoken rule in many workplaces to hide weak-nesses and not confront another team member, or even the team itself in public, brainstorming sessions or SWOT analyses of strengths, weak-nesses, opportunities, and threats may not get you all the information you seek. If that's the case, try using the World Café,[3] a simple yet pow-erful conversational process that encourages people to think together about questions that matter. Appreciative questions posed to the team for their own self-assessment invite exploration and connect partici-pants to *why* they care. As people express their points of view and are listened to carefully, the intelligence of the group becomes accessible and actionable.

This methodology, developed by Juanita Brown, David Isaacs, and their colleagues, is based on the premise that we have the wisdom within us to address even the most difficult challenges. A World Café creates a convivial setting: small, preferably round tables typically sur-rounded by four chairs arranged to allow movement among tables. The tables are covered with white easel paper to encourage doodling. The design of World Café dialogues nurtures democratic group participa-tion, which along with "café etiquette" encourages listening for patterns, insights, and deeper questions.

To begin, a question that matters to the group and is open enough for the members to make the question theirs is posed. After exploring this question for, say, twenty to thirty minutes, a "host" stays at each table, while participants move separately to new tables. This movement among tables occurs several times. With each discussion ideas are pollinated, and key insights, themes, and questions are introduced into new conversations. Members continue recording or drawing key ideas and new connections on the easel paper. After several rounds, the group becomes more visible (often with the support of a graphic recorder), and innovative possibilities for action begin to emerge naturally, leading to greater ownership for change.

In a growing number of café dialogues, the host encourages moments of reflection and journaling, using meditative silence or other practices to enable participants to deepen their individual and collective insights. The award-winning book by Brown and Isaacs, *The World Café: Shaping Our Futures Through Conversations That Matter,* provides detailed guidance and stories of the many ways in which the World Café has helped groups around the globe deal with challenging or pressure-filled issues.

TWO

DON'T BELIEVE EVERYTHING YOU THINK

Moving Beyond the Limitations of Your Personality Type

The willingness to own up to the fictional nature of our story is where the healing begins.

—Peter Block, *Community: The Structure of Belonging*

n the mid-eighties, Jack, the CEO of a tech start-up company, was going to New York City on business for the first time. As this was before Mayor Giuliani reduced the city's crime rate, his friends not only told him about some terrific happening places to visit, they also warned him not to walk through Central Park at night. Jack, a six-foot ex-college football player, thanked them, but they knew he'd ignore their warning. Jack prided himself on being in control of any situation.

One evening, he was rushing back to his hotel room for an important business call when he found himself at the entrance to the park. Although Jack remembered his friends' caution, he decided to take a short-cut through the park, and, wary of the danger, he walked briskly towards the exit. Two blocks from the exit, he collided with a man half his size. They apologized to one another and went their separate ways. As Jack reached the exit, on an instinct, he felt for his wallet. It wasn't there. He spun around and raced after the man. When he caught up with him, he grabbed him by his lapels and demanded the wallet. The man said nothing and meekly did as he was told. Jack, now late for his phone call, returned to his hotel. When he arrived, there was his wallet lying on the dresser. He had just mugged this little guy.

Each of us has at some time reacted inappropriately under pressure. When our minds speak, we listen and rarely question what it tells us. After all, it is *our* mind, so it *must* be telling us the truth. Although we would never fall twice for the same con another person played on us, our own minds con us repeatedly.

How you react greatly depends on the mental patterns that shape your personality or psychological type. These patterns, which include but are not limited to core motivations, habits of paying attention, coping style, and defense mechanisms, are based on a worldview or core belief unconsciously established in childhood. As there are no perfect parents, children intuitively find a way to ensure the two things that are essential to their well-being—safety and love—in an environment that at times may feel threatening. Eventually, these patterns become imprinted in the brain, part of its software.

Your worldview is the core belief that filters your perceptions, colors your interpretations of the world, and limits you from thinking and responding in new ways. Whether or not you realize it, your worldview informs your business view, decisions, and actions. As you will see, at times your worldview is helpful; at other times, it limits you and creates pressure.

The various descriptions that follow come from the Enneagram, an ancient tool for self-knowledge that was given psychological form in the twentieth century by Oscar Ichazo. The Enneagram describes nine basic personality types, each with its own worldview, natural talents, limitations, assumptions, and expectations—its own unique ways of thinking, behaving, and being. Each type has its own emotional driver or motivational force. As a result, each has its own style when it comes to doing business.

Undoubtedly, you'll recognize yourself and many of your colleagues in these descriptions, although not everything will apply to you or to them because, while our worldview never changes, as we develop, some of these tendencies are modified and no longer control us as they once did. Yet, because they are imprinted on our nervous systems, when the pressure is great enough, they sometimes reemerge.

NINE BASIC PERSONALITY TYPES: THEIR IMPACT AT WORK

Although the Enneagram is a comprehensive system, my purpose here is not to provide a thorough description of the model, but rather to increase your awareness of the worldview and coping style of each and to help you identify your personality type. With this knowledge, you may or may not be able to stop your initial reaction when you are under pressure, but you can prevent it from getting out of control. It gives you the option to shift to a more neutral perspective where your vision is clearer and you feel more relaxed and in control of yourself. In subsequent chapters, I will discuss each type's stress and anger triggers.

Note, too, that one type is not better or worse than another, and, although experts provide slightly different explanations of the worldviews, I learned these from Helen Palmer,[1] a noted expert on the Enneagram.

Type 1: The Perfectionist

All my life I believed that unless I was perfect I would not be loved.

—Jane Fonda, actor

Jessica is the COO of a small medical supply company. Although both of the company's owners are involved in the business, one of them lives in another country; the other focuses much of his time on his medical practice. Thus, most of the day-to-day operations and decisions fall on Jessica, who has high standards and is committed to growing the business. Jessica usually works late and often on weekends.

When I met her, the job's demands and pressures were getting to her, and she was becoming resentful of her bosses for making her carry most of the load; she was increasingly impatient—at times outright angry—with them. The owners knew that many employees had resigned because of Jessica's critical management style, but, when she aimed her anger at them, the owners were shocked. Genuinely concerned about her, they hired me to coach her.

As an Enneagram Type 1, Jessica represents the good child who was criticized severely and, therefore, felt compelled to work towards perfection. This belief equates love with being good and being good with being right; therefore, Type 1s tend to be black or white thinkers. In the workplace, they may be the Total Quality Management experts or teachers who want to improve you. They are the ethical leaders; they follow the rules without cutting corners and put what they should do ahead of their own pleasure. They fear making a mistake or that they won't be good enough. Thus, they work doubly hard to prove their worth, are very organized, and prefer a solid plan to winging it. As perfectionists, they tend to judge not only themselves but also others harshly. Because they often think that other people can't do things as well as they can, delegating is often challenging.

Through coaching, Jessica learned to ask for what she wanted and, to her delight, her bosses took on more responsibility. Instead of soldiering on when the pressure was too great, she began treating herself better. Once she softened her tough stance towards herself, her relationships became more positive; she became a better manager, better able to delegate and handle the enormous demands of her job.

Put yourself in the Type 1's shoes. Imagine the pressure you would feel if you had to be perfect all the time.

Type 2: The Giver

One of the deep secrets of life is that all is that is really worth doing is what we do for others.

—Lewis Carroll, author, *Alice's Adventures in Wonderland*

Jackson, the senior vice president of an R&D division, is smart, experienced in both operations and R&D, and a courageous, ethical leader. A number of years ago he hired me to help him develop his leadership team into a collaborative, emotionally intelligent unit.

I noticed that despite his good intentions, Jackson was getting in the way of collaboration by stepping in when his leaders had issues with each other. As the benevolent patriarch, instead of insisting they work things out among themselves, he encouraged them to seek his help. I helped him recognize what he was doing and focus instead on his own needs. We were then able to train his team on how to hold difficult conversations; as a result, the team worked more effectively together.

Jackson is a Type 2 exemplar. As children, they intuited that to be loved they must be needed, that people depended on their help. Type 2s want to be liked; they seek approval by being extremely sensitive to the needs of others. They cope by moving towards people, so that their personal needs are fulfilled by being needed. This protects them from their fear of not being loved or valued.

In the workplace, Type 2 leaders bring out the best in others. They are friendly, compassionate, high energy, empathetic, and make others feel special. Highly developed 2s serve the greater good without thinking about what's in it for them. Yet, sometimes their help, which they may offer generously, is not truly altruistic. In an unrecognized way Type 2s might bring credit on themselves by putting their employees in the spotlight and helping them shine. Since so much of their attention is focused on what others think, feel, and want, Type 2s may not be as keenly aware of their own thoughts, feelings, wants, and motivations. They have a need to please and thus have difficulty setting boundaries. In fact, they may spend so much time helping others that it may be hard to get their own work done. Yet, when they are at their best, Type 2 personality types are accountable for their own passions and desires.

Think about any Type 2s you know. How does their search for others' approval and value inform their work and add pressure to their lives?

Type 3: The Performer

Winning isn't everything. It's the only thing.

—Vince Lombardi, football player, coach, and businessman

What do Jack Welch, Michael Jordan, and Tony Robbins all have in common? Each of them exemplifies success, personal accomplishment, high performance, salesmanship, image, self-promotion, fast action, money, and status. Each of them is also a Type 3 personality. Type 3s are the competent, positive thinking role models whose lives demonstrate what belief in one's self can generate. They are goal oriented and willing to put in the time and work to be the best they can be. Just don't ask them to be self-reflective or spend time in emotional intelligence classes. As workaholics they are too busy and don't see the value in examining their inner life. Instead they manage by setting challenging but attainable objectives and taking moderate risks. They are process and task oriented, and don't mind cutting corners to be efficient. They want to make a good impression on people and are often friendly, personable, and polite. They also are serious competitors.

As children, Type 3s perceived that the world values a champion and rewards people for what they do, not who they are. They noticed that they got attention, love, and approval when they succeeded, and so developed a coping strategy in which failure was not an option. The core desire of Type 3s is to feel worthwhile, acceptable, and desirable; their core fear is that they are without value apart from their achievements.

In the workplace, Type 3s strive to be the most valuable player, the employee of the month, or the top sales producer. Just show them the structure and the rules of the game and watch them race to the goal. I am reminded of a bank executive who, upon recognizing his boss's love of empowerment, championed the concept throughout the organization, and was honored for it. In reality, he couldn't care less about empowering others. He told me, "Whatever the next flavor of the month is, I'll get behind it, too."

Type 3s are chameleons who take on whatever image is necessary for their professional success and believe that that image is truly who they are. By suspending real emotions and needs and replacing them with feelings that successful people are alleged to have, they live in an often unrecognized state of self-deception. When genuine feelings do arise, they bury them in work and when they receive negative feedback from others, they usually discount it.

Although their worldviews set them up to be winners, imagine the pressure they must feel having to prevent failure, maintain their image, and guard against true feelings that might derail their success.

Type 4: The Romantic

Always be a first-rate version of you, rather than a second-rate version of somebody else. —Judy Garland, singer/actor

When the company Gary worked for as the senior vice president of PR was sold to a Fortune 100 company, a new CEO came on board. While other executives were keeping their heads down and playing it cool, Gary sometimes would dramatically and emotionally confront his new boss about certain decisions that he felt downgraded the elite brand he helped to create. Gary figured he had nothing to lose since in his mind the CEO wouldn't recognize his extraordinary creativity, and he would probably be the first to be fired. Six months after the CEO came on board he fired everyone on his executive team except Gary. When Gary asked him why he still had a job, the CEO responded, "You were the only one who was willing to passionately fight for your point of view."

Gary is an exemplar of the Type 4 personality. At their best, Type 4s are emotionally deep, introspective, and self-revealing. Their creative spin slices through the conventional, and they are able to cut to the heart of the matter. They consider themselves special and assume that others don't understand them. Since their identity is based on being unique, they are attracted to the elite and repelled by the ordinary. Type 4s thrive when they are recognized by leaders in their fields and want people to solicit their opinions and ideas, but they may be melancholic, self-absorbed, envious, and impossible to please.

Driven by their emotions, Type 4s at work strive to be the star. They perform best when the energy is high and the risks are great when they go for broke, which keeps them emotionally engaged. They tend to make decisions based as much on their moods as on fact and can be fierce competitors particularly when they think they have something to prove or are being compared to someone they feel is less talented.

Type 4s hide their deepest feeling that something is wrong with them and that they don't measure up. They remember a time in their childhood when everything was going well until something drastically changed—the death of a parent, a divorce, or some change in the family's circumstance. The child sensed that something was missing that others had; they may have felt abandoned. This becomes their worldview and keeps them searching for the perfect circumstance to make them feel loved and whole again. The cup is half empty rather than half full. In the workplace they are more interested in chasing an elusive goal than in achieving it.

Can you see how the worldview and coping strategy of Type 4s inform their business view and the relationships they create? Can you imagine the pressure they must feel having to constantly prove themselves?

Type 5: The Observer

My goal is simple. It is a complete understanding of the universe, why it is as it is and why it exists at all.

—Stephen Hawking, author, *A Brief History of Time*

Jason, a tech support consultant, is so smart, incredibly patient, calm in crisis, and superb at synthesizing information in new ways that you'd think he'd be rolling in money. Not so. His clients love him, but he doesn't have enough customers. Determined to change this, Jason identified his goals, listened to motivational tapes, and wrote a stream of consciousness piece every morning to investigate his mental habits in terms of success. Although his inner work has enhanced his self-awareness, it hasn't gotten him many new jobs. Being an in-his-head, detached kind of guy, he's usually not fully present and lacks the energy to market himself. Promoting himself frightens him. However, on those occasions when his attention settles into his body, he is able to take the action that makes a difference to his bottom line.

As a child, Jason, a Type 5, didn't feel safe around his critical and overbearing mother who continually intruded on him. He thus concluded that the world was invasive and demanded too much. To protect his privacy and resources, Jason withdrew from others and became self-sufficient, taking refuge in his mind where his mother could not get to him. He simplified his needs and accumulated knowledge, which he saw as power. He also learned to delay his emotions, allowing himself to feel only when he was alone. Like other Type 5s, Jason became a keen observer of life, watching the action from a detached point of view.

Type 5s believe that knowledge is power; therefore, they protect and empower themselves by withholding information. They cling to their privacy, creating boundaries and limits to protect them against demands or expectations. Self-promotion, competition, strong demonstrations of feelings, and spontaneity are avoided. Instead, the Type 5s think and analyze in advance to ensure that they are capable and competent. At work, they are known as scholarly, insightful, synergistic, open-minded, and able to concentrate. Fives are the philosophers and challengers of assumptions. Yet, when the action moves away from the cognitive mind and into the world of human connections, emotions, and expectations, Type 5s experience pressure, become uncomfortable, and want to leave. Little wonder that their doors are rarely open and that they don't manage by walking around.

Can you sense the pressure you would feel if your company rolled out an emotional intelligence, collaboration, or employee engagement initiative, and you were expected to not only get on board but to encourage your associates to do so as well?

Type 6: The Trooper

Only the paranoid survive. — Andrew Grove, former CEO of Intel

Frannie received the same email invitations as everyone else on her leadership team, yet she never really felt included in the meetings and social events. Doubting her team's commitment to include her, she complained a great deal, often to her kind boss who listened and passed her tissues when she cried. Although she was an excellent troubleshooter—a skill her team needed—her self-doubt and tendency to look for people's hidden agendas kept her from feeling secure. Over time, her negativity made her teammates not want to work with her. Thus, she lost the support she once had and dearly craved.

Frannie is a Type 6. As children, the Type 6s lost faith in authority when a parent or someone in high esteem let them down. Typical family histories include a parent who didn't keep promises, an alcoholic who couldn't be counted on, or a family filled with secrets, intrigue, and collusion that led the child to see the world as threatening and dangerous and to become suspicious of people, particularly those in authority.

Two types of coping strategies emerge from this core belief. The phobic type obeys authority, seeks a strong protector, and tries to escape perceived threats and dangers. Counter-phobic types rebel against authority and do their own thing. Yet the core desire of both types is to find security and support.

At work, Type 6s have the capacity for great self-sacrifice, are persevering and intuitive, and don't need immediate success. They are loyal associates who are fully committed when the cause is worthy. When their tendency to see behind the scenes is put to good use, they can be great team players, troubleshooters, and builders of coalitions. However,

Type 6s can be so engaged in playing devil's advocate that paralysis by analysis sets in and thinking replaces doing. They are plagued with self-doubt. As they believe that success will draw the attention of hostile authorities, Type 6s, who would like to be high-performing Type 3s, tend to self-sabotage just when success is near.

Put yourself in the Type 6's shoes. Imagine the pressure you might experience if you had to navigate a world you perceived as threatening and dangerous.

Type 7: The Epicure

My motto is: More good times. —Jack Nicholson, actor

Driven by a vision of a nonprofit community that stands together and thus stands stronger, Alan has developed a model that others in his state want to replicate. His innovative, optimistic spirit inspires other agencies, both large and start-up small, to join his collaborative network. Together, agencies share resources, opportunities, backroom tech, and administrative services, and use their combined leverage to influence county officials.

Alan, a visionary Type 7, sees how seemingly different information connects and brings it together in a highly original and coherent way. He is a skilled networker, jack-of-all-trades, and cheerleader, who has his fingers in lots of pies. But don't expect him to be on top of all the details or get to a meeting on time. Alan is a big picture person who can go off on tangents and change his mind if a more exciting project comes along. Permanent commitments are not his strong suit; he likes to keep his options open. When he is juggling too many projects, he often procrastinates and tends to talk more than do. Yet, he easily charms people to enroll in his cause and gets them to do the mundane tasks that bore him and which he considers beneath him. Thus, in just a few years he has significantly grown his agency and his reputation as one who serves the greater good.

If he overpromises sometimes or tells people what they want to hear, it's because he dislikes conflict. Alan likes being happy and wants to keep others happy as well. That this habit protects him from pain, fear, or deprivation doesn't dawn on him. When I told him that his positive attitude was driven by his worldview, he disagreed, and told me that he had a very happy childhood. It was only after he thought more about it that he realized his childhood wasn't as happy as he claimed.

Type 7s either experienced a trauma—such as abandonment, divorce, abuse—or were painfully ignored. Either way, as frightened children, they sensed that the world was limiting, frustrating, and painful. To cope, Type 7s engage in pleasurable activities and fascinating future options that protect them from facing a darker reality.

Type 7s like to bring fun into the workplace and are masters at reframing limited or negative situations into positive scenarios. They are great at brainstorming but not comfortable making the final decision, which ends future possibilities. Though they may rise up the ladder, they have issues with authority—their own and others'. Thus, they prefer egalitarian workplaces. Convinced of their special value, they reject and can be quite defensive of others' feedback when it goes against their self-perception. Type 7s can run shallow, afraid of exploring feelings that threaten their happy outlook.

Can you imagine then the pressure the Type 7s must feel when deadlines approach, there are constraints, or they are forced to face their own limitations?

Type 8: The Boss

You have to think anyway, so why not think big?

—Donald Trump, businessman

Jerry is a chemist and director of a laboratory that produces household products. Known in the industry for his many patents, younger scientists want to work in his lab to learn from him. Jerry is a tough boss with high standards who wants things done his way. If you pass his many tests, he is a loyal and protective boss. However, if you ask questions that he considers irrelevant or stupid, he is dismissive and at times cruel. Jerry communicates forthrightly and expects everyone to tell him the truth and to keep him informed. If you fail to inform him totally, he will feel betrayed and become enraged. However, if you follow his rules, he is a kind, generous, and caring boss.

Jerry is an exemplar of Type 8s, who experienced injustice, such as emotional, physical, or sexual abuse, and/or were rejected when they were weak and respected when they were strong. From this experience, the Type 8s formed a belief that the world is unjust, where the powerful take advantage of others' innocence. Good things, they conclude, go to those who take control. Type 8s' greatest fear is of being controlled or harmed by others, so they develop a coping strategy to protect themselves and others by imposing their own truth and hiding their vulnerability. They may confuse their self-serving version of the truth with the objective truth, and can be quick to blame and punish others for injustices, deceptions, or manipulations. Type 8s tend to see things in all-or-nothing polarities.

They are also extremely responsible, like big challenges, and fight injustice. They are courageous, strategic, structured, unpretentious, decisive, and self-assertive. Although Type 8s are a force to be reckoned with, can you image the pressure they must feel having to always be in control and vigilant against injustice, betrayal, and harm? Think about the Type 8s you work with; does their worldview inform how they do business?

Type 9: The Mediator

> *I decided early on just to accept life unconditionally. I never expected it to do anything special for me, yet I seemed to have accomplished far more than I had ever hoped. Most of the time it just happened to me without my ever seeking it.* —Audrey Hepburn, actor

Enthusiastically, Jay, the executive director of marketing for a beauty company, sold his boss and team on his plan to launch a new fragrance. However, the closer they came to achieving their objectives, the more he began to doubt the plan. The problem emanated from Jay's subconscious belief that the world wouldn't value his efforts. Without realizing it, he began to sabotage himself by spending his time doing inessential tasks rather than working his plan. As the pressure built, his decisiveness lessened. He began avoiding team members, fearing they would want to pin him down to a course of action. The less focused Jay became, the more his team lost confidence in his leadership. Ultimately, his core belief became a self-fulfilling prophecy when the plan fell short.

Type 9s are extremely likable, trusting, and stable leaders. They are kind-hearted, easygoing, and supportive. They work well in teams and tend to create inclusive work environments. One of their greatest strengths is being able to see all points of view. This makes them excellent mediators. However, this strength can also limit their ability to make decisions. Although they rarely lose their cool, they can be too willing to go along with others to keep the peace. Type 9s dislike conflict and can be complacent. Instead of directly asserting themselves, they will space out or passive aggressively resist others. They focus on others' agendas and whatever needs to be done, which distracts from their personal needs, wants, and priorities.

As children Type 9s felt overlooked and their efforts unvalued. To maintain contact with their parents and to keep the peace, they became sensitive to others' feelings and desires and deadened their own. They sensed it was easier for them to merge with others' feelings than to defy and risk being cut off. In so doing, they lost their will to initiate action; self-observation stopped and self-forgetfulness became their habit. Thus, Type 9s become overly accommodating and learn to substitute real priorities for inessentials and small comforts.

Type 9s express this need in the workplace by maintaining structure and routine. They act through habit rather than initiating change, and tend to go with the flow and/or procrastinate; they may be forgetful about agreements. Often their decisions are based on what worked in the past rather than the specifics of the current situation. Rarely do Type 9s create performance goals for themselves. Instead, they passively prioritize, which leads them to be constantly pulled by the demands of their jobs. They achieve control through stubbornness or by waiting things out. They don't like people telling them what to do.

Put yourself in the Type 9's shoes. Imagine the pressure you would feel if you had to make on-the-spot decisions or confront a problem employee or difficult colleague. Imagine how difficult it would be to make a behavioral change particularly if your boss recommended it. Last, imagine how stressed you would feel if you worked in a high-pressure, fast-changing, competitive environment.

Break Out of Your Personality Box

The more you understand how your personality informs every decision you make and action you take as if you were on automatic pilot, the more you recognize the extent to which you have been boxed in by preconceived limitations and reactions. Table 2-1 summarizes each of the nine worldviews and coping styles. Consider how each type's mental preoccupation and the pressure it causes them can affect a meeting (see Figure 2-1 on page 48).

Table 2-1. Summary of types, worldviews, and coping strategies.

TYPE	WORLDVIEW	COPING STRATEGY
1 **The Perfectionist**	The world is an imperfect place. I strive for perfection.	To be loved, I must be good. To be good, I must be right.

2 **The Giver**	People depend on my help. I am needed.	I move towards people. I fulfill my personal needs by being needed. To get, I must give. To be loved, I must be needed.
3 **The Performer**	The world values a champion. People are rewarded for what they do, not who they are.	I get love and approval by achieving success. Failure is not an option.
4 **The Romantic**	Something is missing. Others have it. I have been abandoned.	I search for an ideal love or perfect circumstances to make me feel loved and whole.
5 **The Observer**	The world is invasive and demands too much from people and gives them too little in return.	I move away from people. I protect my privacy and my resources by withdrawing, minimizing contact, becoming self-sufficient, accumulating knowledge, and simplifying my needs.
6 **The Trooper**	The world is a threatening and dangerous place. I am suspicious of people, particularly those in authority.	*Phobic type:* I obey authority and seek a strong protector. I try to escape perceived threats and dangers, gain security, and avoid hazards. *Counter-phobic type:* I defy authority and security, battle perceived threats and dangers, and face hazards.

7 The Epicure	The world limits, frustrates, and pains people.	I protect myself from limitations and pain by engaging in pleasurable activities and imagining many fascinating future options.
8 The Boss	The world is an unjust place. The powerful take advantage of others' innocence. Good things in life go to those who take control.	I protect myself and others by imposing my own truth and hiding my vulnerability.
9 The Mediator	The world overlooks me and won't value my effort.	I stay comfortable and keep the peace. I substitute inessentials and small comforts for real priorities.

THE NEED TO BE RIGHT

Each personality type believes that their way of seeing the world is objectively correct and that other types are defective versions of their own style. It's as if we each have a slice of what we call reality, but we think our slice is the whole pie and do our best to prove ourselves right.

The more certain we are that our worldview is correct, the more judgmental of others we become. For example, years ago the president and chairperson of an investment banking firm asked me to help resolve a conflict between Sheila, the operations director, and Dave, the sales director. There is an inherent conflict between operations and sales in investment firms; however, in this case, their personality types exaggerated it. Things became so bad each wanted the other fired.

Sheila was a Type 1 personality who led by the book. She was first in the office every morning, arrived punctually to meetings, was extremely detail oriented, and was not very flexible. Since she was in charge of compliance, her qualities matched the job perfectly and she excelled at it.

Figure 2-1. How types and their worldviews can affect a meeting.

Dave was a Type 3 personality; he rarely showed up on time, had outbursts in meetings, and did whatever he thought necessary, within legal, ethical, or moral limits, to get his numbers. Rules did not apply to him. He was brilliant at his job. The brokers loved him because they knew he would go the distance for them. "He doesn't come into the office for days," Sheila complained. "He doesn't keep me in the loop and rarely completes his paperwork. Dave thought Sheila was obsessive compulsive, should relax more, and stay off his back.

I helped them see how they needed each other and how their personality traits were perfect for their respective jobs. I guided them to see the thing they disliked within themselves. Sheila acknowledged a free spirit in her just waiting to be released. Though she was serious at work, at home she was funny and caring. I helped her bring that part of herself to work, and, as she freed herself, her tolerance for Dave's behavior increased.

Dave recognized that Sheila shared his drive for success, and that he, too, lacked tolerance when stockbrokers failed to meet his expectations, and that Sheila was just demanding the same of him. Though they were never fans, they did find a more relaxed and productive way of working together.

When you point a finger judgmentally at someone, there are three fingers pointing back at you.[2] We'd all be better off if we didn't believe everything we thought was absolutely, positively right. I'm not suggesting that we should be indecisive, but rather that we think of our beliefs as preferences instead of tightly locking ourselves in. Preferences allow for freedom of choice and release us from our mental habits and robotic behaviors. We would no longer have to defend our perspective, but could seriously consider other points of view. By letting go of our rigid, often judgmental stance, we gain the flexibility and compassion to understand that the other people's behavior grows out of a philosophy that makes perfect sense to them. Moving beyond the limiting boundaries and biases of our worldview, we make better decisions, reduce our stress, and enhance our performance.

Consider what may occur at a meeting of the nine types if each of them broke free of their preconceived limitations (Figure 2-2). Sense the ease they would feel without the need to prove their worldview was right. Imagine the collaboration that might occur.

Figure 2-2. The nine types break free of their limitations.

PERSONAL PRACTICE

**HOW DOES YOUR WORLDVIEW SERVE AND LIMIT
YOUR CURRENT CHALLENGE?**

Instructions: To help you see how your worldview informs your business view, answer the following questions:

- What is the primary issue you are currently dealing with in your professional life?
- Describe your worldview.
- How does your worldview limit your ability to manage this issue or create pressure or stress?
- How does your worldview benefit your ability to manage this issue?

APPLICATION FOR TEAMS

**IDENTIFY YOUR TEAM'S WORLDVIEW AND HOW
IT INFORMS THE WORKPLACE CULTURE**

A senior vice president and his team of five talented leaders and his HR generalist were not functioning cohesively, although their potential was extremely high. Upon assessing each of their personality types, we discovered that the boss, two of his leaders, and the HR generalist all were Type 2 personalities. "No wonder I felt there were really two teams, A and B, and that I was one of the Bs," one of the other leaders declared.

With this knowledge, we began to incorporate the perspectives of the remaining types into the team's culture. Frustrated with the team's inefficiencies, the Type 3 leader encouraged the team to show up on time for meetings and become more process oriented. The Type 6 leader inspired the team to become more inclusive and to troubleshoot potential issues before they happened, while the Type 8 leader urged them to take on bigger challenges and to communicate more directly.

Although they still faced issues in working together, by shifting the culture to incorporate the strengths and talents of each type, they became more engaged, productive, collaborative, and happy. They were also more capable of resolving issues because they shared a culture that supported everyone's worldview and the qualities that emerged from these.

Often the culture of an organization, division, or department reflects the personality style of the leader. Some leaders like to hire and/or retain only people who think as they do. In today's uncertain workplace where replicating past successful decisions often doesn't work, you need a holistic way of approaching problems in order to assess and deal with them most effectively. Thus, it's important to include all personality types in your team to reflect the best of their perspectives and qualities within the organizational culture.

▐▐▐▶ PRACTICE: DISCOVER YOUR TEAM'S WORLDVIEW

To identify your team's worldview, step one is for members to discover their personality type. If they do not recognize themselves in the descriptions outlined earlier, I suggest they self-type using the two-question quiz, which can be found in the book, *The Wisdom of the Enneagram,* by Don Richard Riso and Russ Hudson. Other Enneagram assessments are available online.

The next step is to have members identify the different qualities of the culture, for example, efficient, fun, compassionate, strategic, and so on. Next, ascribe the personality type or types that best correlate with that quality. When we think of fun, most people think of Type 7. When we think of strategic, Types 5, 8, and 3 among others come to mind.

When you are finished, look at the distribution of personalities in your culture. Are there more Type 1s and 2s than other types? If so, the culture's view of the workplace and the marketplace will be skewed because it is framing reality narrowly. It may also be stressful for members who are not Types 1 and 2 because they may feel pressured to think and behave in ways that are not aligned with who they are. When you look at the collective, what type or types are missing and how does that affect the organizational culture?

THREE

YOU CAN'T GET THERE FROM *NOT* HERE

Where Is Your Attention?

The greatest warrior is the one who conquers himself.

—Samurai maxim

While in graduate school, a psychiatrist I knew invited me to visit the acute psychiatric ward of Boston State Hospital. I leapt at the opportunity to engage with people whose perspectives on reality were so different from mine. I hoped to expand my understanding of why some people experiencing pressure achieve inner balance while others don't.

As I entered the solarium, I felt my senses heighten. As the patients mingled, some talked to one another; some mumbled or yelled to themselves; and others sat silently, seemingly depressed. More to ease my discomfort than from any thought of doing music therapy class with them, I sat down at a rinky-dink piano and began to sing and play "You Are My Sunshine." Halfway through the first verse, an old man chimed in. Soon, others began singing and the energy in the room lightened.

I immediately plunged into "Amazing Grace." Then I heard it—one of the purest voices I ever heard. A young black woman wrapped her voice around mine, weaving mosaics of sound that expressed the depth of her heart. As I continued to play gospel music and she continued to sing, the other patients seemed touched by her voice and somewhat calmer. As their attention shifted from their thoughts to the music, their behavior changed and they looked as if they had at least temporarily emerged from the prison of their chaotic minds. Later I learned that the young woman who sang so sweetly had not spoken for months. It was then that I understood that consciousness shifting occurs in a heartbeat. Even more important, I understood that *where we focus our attention is crucial to our well-being because it defines our reality moment to moment.*

Attention is focused awareness, which means we harness, shape, and direct it. In focusing awareness, we highlight a thought or aspect of reality, screening out irrelevant information, sensations, and perceptions. Thus, attention steers our lives. Think of Zen student Steve Jobs, whose insistence on filtering out distractions from his products produced innovative objects that were brilliantly simple to use.

The skill of attending is essential to feeling contained, relaxed, and in charge of ourselves, as well as to achieving high performance. Every wisdom tradition begins with learning how to focus attention; every Special Forces training includes attention training; and every successful businessperson is adept at focusing attention.

By the time we've reached adulthood, you'd think we would have learned the ins and outs of focusing attention. Not so. Just try counting the number of breaths you take, and you will notice how quickly you lose count because you are paying attention to something else. When my friend Richard Moon told me, "You can't get there from not here," I knew exactly what he meant.

It doesn't matter where "there" is. You may have your eye on the C-Suite, or be searching for that elusive idea that will produce a product breakthrough, or simply want to get through a speech without forgetting your main points. In every case, even if you achieve your goal, if your attention is on the future or the past instead of centered deeply

A Seed of Truth

"An expert is someone who has succeeded in making decisions and judgments simply through knowing what to pay attention to and what to ignore."

—EDWARD DE BONO

within yourself in the present, your experience will be less than you imagined. You'll miss the colors, the textures, the meaning, and the subtleties of the situation because your attention is not connected to your physical and energetic sensations. You may even miss opportunities. In fact, the more "there" you are, the less able you are to align with and use the pressure that comes with your desire or task. The result is discomfort or stress.

Therefore, the first step in turning pressure from an enemy into an ally is to become aware of your habits of attention.

Voicemail Message:

"It may seem as if I'm never here, but if you think about it, are any of us?"

—Jenny Winford, graphic artist

THE INFLUENCES ON YOUR ATTENTION

There is a constant interplay between forces that catch our attention and our responses to them. Throughout the day, your attention naturally shifts: Sometimes attention is located inside you so you know what you think, feel, sense, need, and want; at other times, it is located outside of you, in another person or situation. Then there are those times when your attention is blended with another's. Each of us, however, has a conscious or unconscious habit of locating our attention in one place more than another. In addition, circumstances also affect where we place our attention.

The other day, the phone rang just as I was about to leave the office for an appointment with a potential client. Instead of letting it go to voicemail, I answered and got involved in a ten-minute conversation.

I dashed out of the office, got onto the freeway and into the fast lane. I was moving at eighty miles an hour when I had to slow down for the car in front of me who was going at seventy, the speed limit. I could feel the tension inside me build; my breathing became shallow, my chest tightened, and I felt myself disconnect from that place deep inside me, which I call "home." As I drove, I kept checking the clock. As the minutes passed, my muscles and energy field contracted in reaction to my self-imposed pressure. I was oriented so energetically forward that I no longer could feel my back. That's when I realized what I was doing to myself and, finally, smiled.

"Come on back, Aimee," I said lovingly to myself. "You don't need to do this to yourself. It's not helping you get there any faster." With that, my body began to soften. In an instant, all the energy streams of my attention reversed course and gathered back inside me. I was "home." Amazingly, after a couple of wrong turns, I arrived at the meeting on time, much more collected and confident than when I departed.

All of us lose our sense of hereness a number of times each day. Sometimes it's just a slight move away from our deepest core; at other times, we are truly gone. Maybe your fuse becomes lit after spending twenty minutes navigating a telephone menu when all you want is a simple answer to your question. Maybe it's the guy who steals the parking spot you've been courteously waiting for that brings out the nasty in you. Each time, if you lose your cool, your smile, and your happy day, you've given your energy and power away. Navigating the ups and downs of people's moods, office situations/politics, and economic uncertainties is challenging. When you add our western culture, which influences how and where we place our attention, the level of mastery you need to stay centered jumps considerably.

The Influence of Culture

Western culture teaches us to focus on what lies in front of us; the opportunities, achievements, and pleasures awaiting us; the to-do list; the dangers and disappointments that may appear at any moment. Our society looks to the future and shies away from the past.

Modern life bombards us with stimuli continually seducing our attention. As I write this, I am sitting on the patio of a happening restaurant on the Intercoastal Waterway in southeast Florida. The comings and goings of the beautiful people on their beautiful boats beckon as the Heat basketball game on one TV competes with MTV on a second screen. From my seat, I can also watch the cook flipping a pizza, and, from inside the restaurant, a rock band blares. It is a circus for the senses, and I haven't yet been served my meal.

Western culture dangles the idea that not only can we have more, but we are also entitled to it. Keeping up the pace of the "good life" can be just as stressful as recognizing that we don't have all we were told we *should* have.

As modern life demands that we attend to more things in less time, we believe we must move faster to accomplish all that life requires. As we do, the pressure builds. Yet, moving faster isn't the answer. Multitasking, neuroscience tells us, compromises our effectiveness. Yet, we race ahead, and before we know it, we have moved away from our center, the place I call "home" or "here." The more we distance our attention from ourselves, the more drained, pressured, and disheartened we feel. Our decisions may become flawed and our relationships stressful. In this state, even when things go our way, life seems hard.

Much of the time, we are so lost in our thoughts or actions that we fail to notice where our attention is located until the pressure wakes us up. To help you recognize when your attention is outside of yourself and to practice bringing it back inside, try the basic exercise that follows.

||||▶ PRACTICE: NOTICING THE DIFFERENCE BETWEEN
HERE AND THERE

While sitting, take a moment to focus your attention outside of yourself on an object (not a person) in the room. Choose something that is not too far away. Let's call this location "there." After you've stared at it for a few moments, you'll probably feel as if there is no distance between you and it. Now reverse the direction of your attention and slowly—frame by frame—bring your attention back inside yourself; the first place it goes is into your eyes. It's similar to fishing: You send your line out—or in this case the beam of your attention—it connects with something, and you slowly reel your line, or attention, back.

Now close your eyes and let them rest in their sockets. You may also see the object in your mind's eye. Let your attention, and, if you see it, the picture of the object, move into the back of your head. Slowly allow your attention to settle down through your body. When it does, the picture will disappear. Imagine that your attention is being pulled down through your spine. As it drops into your chest, notice your breathing. Allow your attention to continue to settle deeper until you are aware of pulling your breath into your lower belly. Take a few moments and continue to sense/feel your lower belly fill up; then slowly let go of the breath. Relax into the chair. Then, trusting your own sense of timing, slowly open your eyes and look again at the object. Whatever you experienced is correct.

* Repeat this experiment two more times. You may not think you are very adept at this or that anything is happening, but do it anyway.
* Each time that you finish, describe the difference in your experience between being "here" and being "there."
* Did your relationship and sense of distance with the object change? If so, how?
* Which location felt more familiar?

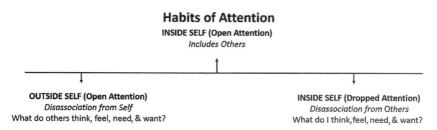

Figure 3-1. Habits of attention.

Attention Outside Yourself

All of us have had the experience of being swept away by something outside of ourselves. Losing ourselves at times in a job, a cause, a situation, a goal, or another person comes with being human. In these moments what is outside feels more compelling than what is inside us and we are affected and perhaps altered by it (Figure 3-1). For example, while watching the trauma of the victims of war on TV, you may temporarily lose yourself in their pain. Or, you may become so angry at your bullying boss that you can't stop complaining and telling stories about him. Or, you may become so influenced by an expert's words that you forget to examine your own opinion. However, once the newscast is over, once we let go of the stories, or once we finally reflect on our own thoughts and values, these journeys outside ourselves fade as the self awakens and beckons us home.

Looked at from a positive perspective, these externally focused experiences may provide an opportunity to discover our empathy, open our minds to new ways of thinking, and sense connections with others that enliven us. However, if losing yourself becomes a way of life, it can compromise your self-esteem, well-being, and sense of integrity.

Luisa, a human resource generalist and a Type 2, is known for being one of the nicest people at the plant. Her coworkers trust her because she is more concerned with helping others than she is in stroking her ego. When we began working together, I was touched by her openness and welcoming nature, and we quickly created a strong partnership.

As I got to know her, I saw that she did not always speak her mind or confront the team about the dynamics that were limiting it. Sometimes, she explained, she didn't notice them; at other times she said nothing because she didn't want to hurt people's feelings. When she did speak her mind, she often apologized first. As a result of her lack of assertiveness and self-confidence, people didn't think of her as a person with much influence. Luisa's attention was so focused on others that she didn't recognize her own worth. In her desire to help, she gave her power away, often without even recognizing it. She had difficulty establishing healthy boundaries for herself and had a hard time saying "No." Little wonder that she often felt exhausted at the end of the day.

Over the five years I partnered with her, I witnessed her transformation. Using the energy principles I describe in this book, Luisa learned to gather her attention back inside, enabling her to listen, value, and trust her instincts. In turn, as her confidence and assertiveness grew, others began to trust her more and her input became very valuable to the senior vice presidents with whom she worked.

Luisa no longer runs away from confrontation or from voicing her opinion. She is still nice, but people sense her confidence and presence. Her internal changes even manifested in her appearance. Never a fashionista, she recently dyed her hair bright white and had it stylishly cut. She now wears fashionable clothes that perfectly reflect her new soft, yet powerful persona. By learning to shift her attention from "there" to "here," Luisa upgraded her identity.

The earlier version of Luisa exemplifies those people who habitually locate their attention inside others. You know if you are one of them if you:

- Are more aware of what others think, feel, need, and want than you are of what you think, feel, need, and want
- Are highly influenced by others' opinions
- Spend too much time and energy trying to change, help, or fix others

- Have difficulty establishing and maintaining personal boundaries
- Think that giving usually requires self-sacrifice
- Have difficulty making decisions, particularly personal ones
- Are overly concerned with what others think about you; whether others like or approve of you
- Lack a sense of groundedness
- Lack ability to be contained within yourself

THE DYNAMICS OF ATTENTION OUTSIDE YOURSELF

If you are unable to break rigid emotional and behavioral patterns that keep you looking outside, it's time to change the energetic ones that precede and determine them.

Before you realize it, what began as a mental interest energetically and then physically pulls you ever so slightly forward. The more outer- or future-directed your attention, the less you will physically sense your back. Thus, you won't feel supported psychologically, emotionally, and physically. In an unconscious effort to regain your sense of balance, you may tense your upper back, shoulders, and neck. As your life energy moves up and out of you, you lose a strong connection with the ground. Once separated from that which nurtures, supports, and empowers you, your ability to attract people and things that are aligned with your needs is compromised. Instead, you may find yourself in a repetitive cycle, attracting people and things that disappoint and hurt you or missing the mark no matter how hard you try. Even when you win, you feel like you exerted a great deal of will and effort. In this future-forward state, it may seem as if you can't catch up with yourself no matter how fast you run. As Figure 3-2 illustrates, that's because you have separated your attention from your physical body and are out of alignment with yourself and the laws of nature.

You can, at any time, reverse the direction of your attention and come home. In the Personal Practice section I'll show you how.

Figure 3-2. Out of alignment.

Attention Inside Yourself: Dropped Attention

Rushing through life stretches my attention outside myself until I reverse the direction and find that deep place within me that I call "home"—those quiet moments, those times when I can hear myself think and feel myself breathe. I get homesick if I am away too much. I long to close the door, turn the phone off, and disengage from the world. A good book calms me; a little self-reflection awakens me; a meditative practice never fails to recharge me.

In these moments, I am self-centered—unwilling to share my energy. Self-absorbed, I may not even notice when someone comes into the room. The show is about me and I not only like it, I need to experience it in all its colors, sounds, and sensations. In this me-with-me world, I can invite the silence that refreshes and realigns me. Without these periods, I would be a shriveled version of myself, unable to contribute to those around me. When I open the door to myself and let people in again, this centered hereness stays with me. I call this experience "dropped" attention because it is dropped inside me; it doesn't include anyone else.

Most of us have had similar experiences. When used to reconnect with yourself, the habit of closing down to the world may deepen your character, lead to a new way of thinking about your concerns, allow you to discover what is deeply hidden within your heart, or hear the whispers of the creative muses.

There are other times when dropping our attention inside us brings less positive results. A man I'll call Peterson was reputed to be one of the smartest people in Silicon Valley. Although many people wanted to share ideas with him, they were intimidated by his brilliance and his aloofness. Sure, he could pull out the right social skills when he needed to, but when it wasn't essential, he didn't bother. People considered him unapproachable.

One day, while walking to the company auditorium to give a speech, he was so wrapped up in his thoughts that he didn't notice a pillar in front of him and walked right into it. People noticed but said nothing, and Peterson gave an extraordinary presentation on the future of technology. Leaving the auditorium, still consumed by his thoughts, he again walked into the pillar. The story got around, and the next day a sign saying "Peterson's Pillar" appeared. From that day on, he was considered approachable. Good thing. Not only did his new connection with people generate more collaboration, it alleviated his loneliness.

Lapses of sensitivity toward others come with being human. However, if this style of attending becomes a habit, then narcissism, arrogance, a false sense of entitlement, loneliness, and inner tension, among other things, may result from a life of self-absorption. When a trusted executive assistant mistakenly deleted important data from her computer, her boss asked, "How can you do this to me?" When an associate started crying in his office, a senior manager lied and told her he had to reschedule the meeting, because he was overwhelmed by her tears and didn't want to show his vulnerability. The good news is that these people self-reference; the bad news is that they are so caught up in their own worlds that they can't understand what others might be experiencing. They would benefit from Stephen Covey's advice to "seek first to understand then to be understood." You know if you are one of those who habitually close down to others if you:

* Put your feelings, needs, and wants before those of others
* Are often unaware of the depth to which your words and actions affect people
* Often believe you must move against others or disengage from them in order to be safe, in control, and get what you want
* Tend to withhold emotionally or energetically
* Are self-absorbed and think that everyone else is too

Sometimes dropping your attention inside yourself is the best choice. However, when self-absorption and disassociation from others become a habit, relationships become difficult and life becomes hard. To loosen

A Seed of Truth

"We grow the aspects of our lives that we feed—with energy and engagement—and choke off those we deprive of fuel. Your life is what you agree to attend to."

—JIM LOEHR

this habit's hold, it helps to understand it from an energetic point of view.

THE DYNAMICS OF DROPPED ATTENTION

Afraid of being intruded upon or controlled by others, people who habitually focus internally keep themselves separate. It may manifest as a closing down to others' points of view, an armoring of the heart, and/or an ongoing mental discourse in which the person observes or projects rather than engages. Some people with this habit avoid or back away to create distance from others. "I don't like giving all of myself at one time," an executive told me. "I like holding some part of me in reserve."

Energetically, the field around such people begins to shrink, as their attention gets located in their heads. The more they attempt to protect themselves through observation and analysis, the more they disconnect from their roots and lose touch with their feelings and/or instincts. As Figure 3-3 illustrates, their reference point is in themselves, but they are no longer emotionally connected.

Influence of Attention Inside Yourself: Open Attention

Loretta, the new senior vice president of marketing, entered the conference room to meet for the first time with her colleagues on the leadership team. Stepping across the threshold, she paused to take stock of the

Figure 3-3. Out of alignment.

room. A few people were deeply engaged in work conversations; others joked with each other; still others sat quietly at the table waiting for the meeting to begin. Since she was the newest member of the team, as the group's team building consultant, I was curious to see how she would handle herself. I immediately noticed her confidence and presence.

Although she could match any one of the people in the room intellectually, she wasn't inside her head. Instead, her attention was deeply inside herself, yet Loretta's soft but powerful energy field seemed to embrace everyone. One by one people sensed her presence and felt her warmth; they smiled or nodded. It seemed that without a word, they felt her acceptance. Even the most contrary and arrogant members seemed to instantaneously shift from their heads to a deeper, less hard-edged place within them. As she walked to her seat, I sensed the energy in the room quiet down and settle. *She is going to be great for the team*, I thought. *She had them at "hello."*

Although we may not recall a situation in which we had as dramatic an effect on others, most of us have felt deeply connected to ourselves yet open to others. Open attention probably occurred when you were deeply listening and seeking common ground with a colleague you liked or when, in your best presentations, you paused to connect with yourself before you spoke and then energetically embraced the audience.

When we connect to ourselves and open to others, our inner strength and capabilities are enhanced. Energy that we used to resist the outside world is freed to engage with others. In this open state, we are more capable of understanding another's perspectives, feelings, and needs and distinguishing them from our own projections, fears, and inadequacies. We are also more attuned to people's intent and can respond faster and more appropriately. In an open exchange, other people's viewpoints and feelings are gifts that move us beyond the constraints of our own experience to show us a larger reality. Once we allow another's energy in, whether it's a thought, feeling, or sensation, we are never the same. It triggers in us what may lie dormant, denied, or unrecognized, and awakens us to a larger sense of ourselves.

When our attention is deep inside us yet open to what is around us, we operate with wisdom—with eyes that see beneath the surface of things and with a compassion that serves to inspire us and others to greatness. In this state, our attention embraces people. We no longer need to fix, change, or judge them; we accept them as they are. The miraculous beauty of this state is that others sense our acceptance and, feeling safe, let go of their pretensions and resistance and are able to contribute their best. As they let go, they reconnect with themselves and mirror back this openness.

Being connected to self and simultaneously open to others is the dynamic system that serves as a doorway to a deeper and easier way of living. Being contained yet open to the world, we can see the long view and are not compelled to act immediately. Rather than spiraling out of control when the winds of change rip through us, we are aligned and supported by the universal laws of nature, and although we may not like what is occurring, we are not victims of it.

What might this experience of being "home" feel like as it deepens? How do we regain our presence when we are thrown off balance by the pressures of life? And how does this depth make our lives easier? In Chapter 4, we'll examine this integrated state. For now, it helps to remember when you are racing to the meeting, or working out in the gym, or sitting down with your loved ones for a meal, to ask yourself, *WHERE AM I? Is my attention here or out there?*

Then sense/feel where you are and if you are not present, or if you are not connected to others when you want to be, *call your attention back. Allow yourself to open*, and remember the mantra that brought Dorothy back to consciousness: *There is no place like home.*

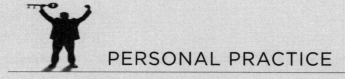

PERSONAL PRACTICE

FREE YOURSELF FROM LIMITED HABITS OF ATTENTION

When you say that you don't have the time to reconnect with yourself, don't believe it. Though you may not be able to go to the gym or take a vacation, you do have a minute here or five minutes there to spend on yourself. As I learned from Julia Cameron, author of *The Artist's Way*, if you don't have the time, steal it. Create rituals that call you back in a heartbeat. They work.

> *You just have to want to;*
> *You just have to practice;*
> *You just have to remember.*

▌▌▌➡ PRACTICE: BREAK FREE

If you tend to place your attention outside of yourself, try this:

1. *Call your attention back inside you.* Like a well-trained dog, expect it to come when you call. All you need to do is ask it, and then act "as if." Throughout your day, call it back so it doesn't get too far away from you: before you turn on your computer; every time you open a door; before you answer the phone; when in the presence of your boss, your lover, your child. *Call it back, call it back, call it back.*

2. *Get into the habit of asking yourself what you think, feel, need, and want.* Make these questions your mantra. Don't wait to ask yourself when you are in a difficult situation; accustom yourself to asking these questions in all interactions and situations. Over time, self-referencing will become a habit.

3. *Use your body as a feedback tool.* Leaning forward—actually, not metaphorically—is not just bad posture; it's a sign that you have located your attention outside yourself. Let go and come back home.

If you tend to place your attention inside yourself and disengage from others, try this:

- Ask your attention to come out and play. Say YES to engaging and being fully present. Pretend your whole being is smiling.
- Get into the habit of asking yourself what other people think, feel, need, and want. If you are not sure, ask.
- To break the hold of your self-restraint, MOVE. Take a walk, stretch, pace, or dance. Movement opens up your energy field and breathes new life into you. Physical movement develops a flexibility that has the potential of opening your mind, heart, and instincts.
- See something good in others and praise them for it. This shifts your attention from the judgments of your mind and creates a heart connection with others.

APPLICATION FOR TEAMS

FOCUS ON WHAT'S CRITICAL

Like individuals, organizations have habits of attention. Some habits, such as Jobs's practice of going deep and simplifying, serve an organization well. Other habits, such as maintaining policies that are no longer relevant or focusing on the inessential, leak the organization's energy/power.

One of the greatest stressors occurs when busy associates do not know the organization's strategy and can't determine what assignments or aspects of their work are truly crucial to the organization's success. Without understanding how their work fits into the overall picture, they don't know if what they are doing makes a difference. Work may then become mechanical, just a series of tasks that causes people to lose their passion for it. To minimize this, the first thing an organization or team needs to do is to *determine what is of most importance.* This is called "mission critical."

In most companies, the C-Suite determines the objectives, and the senior executives tell their team leaders, who in turn tell theirs. By the time the message gets down to the frontline workers, it has been filtered so many times that it's hard to know what is real. The bottom thinks they know the strategy, but they don't know what may have been added or subtracted. As Tim Arnst, senior vice president of human resources for Universal Studios Parks and Resorts stated:

> *"The key is to ensure everyone is aligned to the overall business strategy. It doesn't matter if we take different paths to get there. The communication of that strategy is critical and helps the team understand the role they play in it.*
>
> *"To ensure alignment, I first need to understand the overall business objective and ultimately the business strategy as communicated by the executive team. Then I create an HR strategy that supports the business strategy. Recently, instead of just communicating the HR strategy to my senior HR people and having them pass on my message, I brought the entire human resources group, from my VPs to my coordinators, together for a strategy session. I wanted them to hear it straight from the horse's mouth. . . . 'I'll tell you what I think is important and also why it is critical to the overall business success and you will get a chance to respond . . . Once we all agree . . . it will take a lot of stress off. . . .' I talked about where we were going and what I saw each division doing to get us there. I shared the three critical things I felt we needed to get done in each*

*area and how it aligned to the overall business strategy. We went through every area in HR ... 'Let me show you how all the pieces are going to fit together,' I said. 'We've got a set target and we'll get all of these things done. We will be successful and here's how.' I could see them think-*ing, I see how I fit; I see how I am a part of this bigger thing. *And the bigger thing is not just HR it's the business.*

"... I could see the relief on their faces. Many people thanked me and told me how helpful it was to understand the whole plan."

FOUR

FUNCTION FROM YOUR CENTER

Preserving Your Integrity Under Pressure

The primary task of a leader is the mastery of his or her energy.

—Peter Drucker

Natalie, a media relations director, shared this experience:

"One day, an emergency call came in for my boss who wasn't around, so I took the call. A construction crew working on a major bridge accidentally cut through the flanges that keep the bridge steady. Traffic crossed the bridge for twenty-four hours before they realized what they had done. Once they found the problem, they ran tests and discovered that the integrity of the bridge was compromised and closed the bridge to traffic. Thousands of people could have died if that bridge had fallen. I sent my department and other nonessential employees home so they wouldn't have to answer any questions. I remained on hand to answer questions from the public and media.

"I often had to put a positive spin on things when talking with the press; however, this situation made me physically sick. I couldn't sleep. My psoriasis acted up and my scalp was bleeding. I did what my boss and his higher-ups told me to do yet I was concerned that if the truth leaked out, my job would be the one on the line. To protect myself, I documented everything. My team coped by joking, but I felt awful about lying to the press. There were times though when I wouldn't do what my boss wanted me to. I knew saying outright that I wouldn't do it was unacceptable, so I'd tell him that I was afraid I would say the wrong thing, and, if he was available, that it would be better for him to talk to the press. Most of the time, I made him tell me what he wanted me to say. In my mind, I would tell myself, *I'm just the messenger.*"

Natalie's organization got away with the deception, and her boss was comfortable with her performance. However, Natalie paid a price in terms of her health and self-esteem. Who she defined herself to be and how she was required to act were out of alignment, and, as a result, she lost her integrity. Soon after this experience, she quit her job.

Few of us will ever have to deal with issues of such magnitude, yet each of us is called upon at work to make decisions and take action when we are under pressure. Although you can't control other people's decisions and actions, you do have a choice between becoming a victim of the situation and preserving your integrity.

The word *integrity* is often defined as a consistency of values, beliefs, and actions. Sounds simple, but it's not always. Integrity has another meaning, which is the condition of being whole and complete, and it is this broader definition that I am using in this chapter. When you are whole and complete, it is much easier to decide and act on what you truly believe and value. Wholeness implies that all the parts of you—your mind, emotions, body, and energy field—operate as one, aligned and unimpaired. In this context, I will introduce you to the process of centering, which, when experienced deeply, positions you to act with integrity and authenticity even when times are the toughest.

Natalie suffered on both counts. She wanted to act with moral integrity but decided she had to make compromises, and, because Natalie's vision of herself and what she had to do to preserve her job were out of alignment, she became a victim of the situation. As a result, she paid a high price physically and emotionally.

FINDING BALANCE UNDER PRESSURE

In this chapter we will focus on centering and grounding, the second and third elements of the inner map to stresslessness (for a refresher, see the Introduction). We'll describe the levels of experience, identify the benefits they provide, and map out what you can do to deepen your center/ground experience so you remain balanced and whole under pressure. Let's begin with the link between maintaining our integrity and the mind/body relationship.

Integrity and the Mind/Body Relationship

As Natalie's story demonstrates, the damage that occurs when we lose our integrity manifests on physical and emotional levels. Without our conscious intent, the body serves as our honesty meter, reacting to our mind's rationalizations and challenging us to assess our decisions and actions.

Elmer and Alyce Green tell us in their classic book, *Beyond Biofeedback*, "Every change in the physiological state is accompanied by an appropriate change in the mental-emotional state, conscious or unconscious, and conversely every change in the mental-emotional state, conscious or unconscious, is accompanied by an appropriate change in the physiological state. The body affects the mind, the mind affects the body, and then the new body affects the mind and so on."[1]

If you are unaware of your emotions, physical sensations, and intuition, or if your conditioned mind is so invested in your point of view, you either won't notice your body's signals or you'll try to ignore them. Over time you might develop a stress-related disease. However, if you are attuned to your mind/body, as Natalie was, you can make another choice.

Most people try to change their behavior and reduce the stress using insights, self-talk, and affirmations. Sometimes this works; often it doesn't because personality, which is like your mind's software, is pre-programmed. Thus, it is often easier to go through the back door, so to speak, by shifting the body in order to change your thoughts.

Reduce Stress by Aligning the Three Perceptual Centers

Your body has three main perceptual centers—your head, heart, and *hara* (located in the lower belly). Wherever you place your attention affects your experience and draws your energy to that location. Throughout the course of the day your attention shifts from one to another, but if you are like most people, your attention resides more often in one of these, and that generally is in your head.

The cognitive mind enables us to think, analyze, synthesize, and evaluate information. However, living in your head cuts you off from your emotions, bodily sensations, and intuition; therefore, you may not notice the nuances of a situation or recognize how your words affect people emotionally. When life is primarily about thought, you lose the richness of experience. Relationships may not be as deep; you may feel lonely. Pressure and stress experienced by the mind lead to overthinking, worrying, making false assumptions, doubts, Pollyannaish optimism, and/or stories of doom and gloom.

For this reason, some business gurus suggest living from your heart. When your attention resides in your heart, you feel connected to everything around you. You feel compassionate, giving, and kind. You care about your coworkers and want to motivate, empower, and inspire them. Relationships may flourish that may enhance your influence. Sounds ideal, that is, until you get carried away by your emotions and lose sight of the bigger picture.

For example, I asked teachers and administrators at a childcare center what made them glad. "We are like a family," they responded proudly. This network of caring, this joint attention to the heart, maintains them through hours of listening to noisy children, through countless renditions of "The Wheels on the Bus," and through stacks of paperwork. "It's my calling," many of them told me. Yet, they have difficulty marrying their good work with the business of running a multimillion-dollar nonprofit organization. Thus, when the CEO of this nonprofit announced, "We can't continue to care for infants. The program is expensive to run, we are losing money, and we have to raise $1.8 million just to keep our doors open," few were open to hearing it and no one offered proactive suggestions. Sometimes leading from the heart shuts down common sense.

The third perceptual center, known in aikido as *hara* (meaning "one point"), is located a few inches below the belly button, which is your center of gravity. Here, the weight of your upper body and torso is channeled down through your legs into the ground. More than just a physical location, *hara* pulsates with energy. Meditation students are taught to breathe from here in order to relax the body and experience finer states of consciousness; singers learn to breathe into it for richness of sound, endurance, and control; and martial artists use it to learn to move. Psychologist Richard Strozzi-Heckler describes it as "the place from which we are both inwardly calm and outwardly ready for action."[2]

Focusing your attention in your *hara* ignites the process of centering, which occurs when the three centers are fully integrated and balanced. When you are centered, you are able to draw on a wealth of information derived from your cognitive mind, heart, and body, which allows you to deal with enormous pressure and invites breakthroughs and mastery.

HOW IT FEELS TO BE CENTERED

You don't have to be a disciple of yoga or a New Age philosophy to experience your center. Everyone does. In fact, centering often occurs accidentally while walking, listening to music, or exercising. Although we tend to think of it as a particular experience, centering is an ongoing mind/body process that gets stronger the more you practice it. Centering operates on three levels—the subjective, objective, and universal. However, for our purposes, we will focus only on the first two.

Let's begin with the subjective or personal. Jim Detwiler, an executive director of packaging, spent eight years in high school and college running sprints and jumping hurdles, which was physically demanding. He found his center when the race began:

> "I would wipe everything out of my mind. I felt relaxed, calm, and confident. Before the gun, I was like a coiled spring ready to go. I wasn't in an explosion mode, more like that place just before it. I felt stable, quiet, focused, and my listening was heightened. Once the gun went off, I shot out. Everything was in slow motion. My breathing was controlled which helped keep me centered. When I ran, my whole body acted as one unit. I never looked at the other runners but always ran my own race."

In this first level of centering you *feel balanced, relaxed, and present*. Your perceptions expand and you feel more self-contained. Your breath is located deep in the lower belly, and everything that was out of alignment (the shoulders that were raised to carry your burdens, the slight leaning forward that came from racing around with your attention outside yourself) comes back into alignment so your mind and body act as one unit. That's the integrity Jim noticed in his mind/body when he ran.

Martine, a Type 5 personality, shared the following:

> "Much of the time I live in my head. However, when I'm centered I can think, but my mind is not running me. My heart feels open and I have a sense of aliveness that I lack when I'm in my head. I'm not overly emotional or frantic. Instead of breathing high into my chest, my breath is low in my belly. When I'm cen-

tered, I feel confident, spacious, and relaxed. I'm more intuitive and able to take action more easily."

Centering increases your awareness, energy, and confidence. You trust yourself more and act decisively. Your presence grows, and people notice you. However, at this level of centering you may or may not be willing to maintain your integrity by speaking up when you disagree with your supervisor or organization, and your goals are not necessarily in alignment with what is best for you and others. It depends on how locked in you are to the worldviews, coping styles, and beliefs of your conditioned mind. However, as your centering practice deepens, your reference point shifts.

How Centering Opens You to Possibilities

With practice, the experience of centering shifts from the subjective to the objective. Instead of being rigidly ruled by your conditioned mind, its tight boundaries soften, and you have more options in how you respond to people and situations. Philip, an executive trust banker, describes it this way:

> "Being centered seems to be a heightened level of attention and awareness that is less tied to my conceptions and ego. Being centered gives me several seconds that I can use to determine a course of action. It is being in the moment as things are unfolding, and it may lead to decisions that are other than what my surface personality has so often chosen."

As centering frees you from the bonds of your conditioned mind, your energy expands to include others. You recognize that center is not just in you; you are in an expanded center, which provides a spaciousness and ease. Thus, instead of reacting to slights or threats, you remain composed and emotionally detached and, therefore, do not to take them personally; even if they were meant personally, you respond in a calm, compassionate, and effective manner. The stronger your center, the more equipped you are to handle conflict with integrity.

Peter, a senior vice president of quality for a global company, confided:

> "When I'm centered, I feel it from my toes up; I stand and walk taller. My outlook on life is different. I may know the guns are aimed at me, but that's okay because I know I'm in the right place and can maintain my integrity. When I'm off-center, I sense something's not right. I don't feel well; I'm overly tired; I'm focused on the wrong thing. As a leader, I feel secure in the fact that I work with people I trust and who trust me. I know we have each other's back. I'm secure in myself yet have the humility to invite others to help me make decisions. Being centered also means that when I make a decision I weigh all points of view. Very few problems are one-dimensional. You need to look at them from the business side, the legal side, the people side, etc. When you are off-center, you eliminate points of view that don't fit in with yours."

"Centered" at this level means "grounded in your deeper values and connections with others." When centered, you are authentic. You no longer need to be what others—the organizations to which you belong or your culture—expect you to be. You can be yourself and, without fanfare, acknowledge and act from your inherent value and uniqueness. *The more centered you are, the more integrity you have, and therefore, the harder it is for you to be torn asunder by self-doubt, fear, and high-pressure situations.*

Peter continued:

> "I'm not a great fan of marketing spin. I believe we have to stand behind our word. So, when I received a blatantly poor quality

shipment from overseas, I couldn't look the other way. Our lawyers said that since we knew about the problems, which could harm people, the company would be liable. I wrote a letter to the CEO and to the new president, saying that I wouldn't release the product. I knew that in not playing ball with the global heads of quality, R&D, and marketing, all of whom were aware of the defect, there would be personal consequences, but it was the right thing to do and I did it.

"The CEO, who had been unaware of the issue, stopped the launch at huge cost. However, the only people held responsible were the second- and third-tier leaders, who lost their jobs, and not the senior leaders. Although I was just trying to protect him, the president was furious that I went over his head. The company lost tens of millions, but we protected the integrity and value of the brand. A few years later, the global leaders reorganized, and I was told they no longer needed a senior level manager in the U.S.

"I would do it all again. You can't let the pressure of politics stop you from doing what you know is right. As my family depended on my salary, it would have been a devastating time for me to be out of work. Yet, I knew that if I made an unethical decision, I couldn't undo it or make up for it later. If I went along with the program, what would I be teaching my kids, and how would I face my team? My team thought I was either gutsy or crazy, but decided that if I could stand up for quality, they would too."

Centering places you in the midst of the action and guides you by expanding the clarity of your perceptions. As centering deepens, you experience it as not just something within you that divides and balances two halves such as the right and left sides of your body or two opposite points of view; instead, *centering gives rise to the two halves, includes them both, and, at the same time, is something unique in itself.* Applying this level of center

A Seed of Truth

"Today's mighty oak is just yesterday's nut
that held its ground."
—DAVID ICKE

to business strategy provides a third way that is much more effective than either fighting with or succumbing to the competition.

To see how applying this level of centering to a business problem works, consider this example. When Cellular One was starting up in San Francisco during the 1980s, they were competing with giant GTE for market share. GTE had a two-year head start, had opened a significant number of retail stores, and was in the process of educating the public about cellular. There was no way tiny Cellular One could compete with them on their turf. From its inception, the Cellular One team, headed by Jim Dixon, held retreats led by consultants Chris Thorsen and Richard Moon. They practiced slow-motion aikido and dialogued about the principles they learned and possible applications to their business strategy.

At one retreat, the team practiced multiple force attack. With many people simultaneously pressuring one person, that person doesn't seem to have very many options and it's easy to feel hemmed in. Yet as they practiced, the centering of whomever was attacked deepened, and the person learned to join with an attacker's force and find the open space within the field of attackers, which enabled the person to deal with the multiple attacks strategically, not just tactically.

Their dialogue sessions then focused on applying what they had learned to create a successful strategy for handling the multiple forces in the marketplace. They decided to take advantage of GTE's advertising initiative, and let them educate the public about cellular, while they looked for open spaces in the marketplace that GTE had missed or ignored. By teaming up with existing electronic retailers like Radio Shack, they created a large, secondary distribution network. On the day Cellular One formally entered the marketplace, they had 70 percent of the market share.

Centering Under Pressure

Our experience of center shifts with the pressures that are exerted on us, which lets us adapt to our inner and outer environments. We are constantly re-centering ourselves, though, at times, the shifts may be too subtle for us to notice.

Put under enough pressure, each of us reacts by hardening and pushing forward (attacking), weakening and collapsing, spacing out, or distracting ourselves. When we push forward, we resist the pressure by attacking the problem or person. When we collapse, we absorb the pressure and become its victim. When we space out or distract ourselves, we may say we don't care, drink excessively, or compulsively shop. In this way, we refuse to acknowledge the pressure even though our mind/bodies are negatively affected by it.

Although each of us tends to react in a particular way, we also employ each of these ways of reacting at different times. One is no better or worse than another; they are all limited. In time, whichever way we react ultimately sends us in the opposite direction. For example, we may speak harshly to an associate and then feel guilty or remorseful. At the height of a success, we may exude enthusiasm only to feel let down or sad later. Under pressure, our emotions, perspective, and physical state flip-flop until our energy comes to rest at our natural center. This pendulum swing occurs naturally. As physics tells us, every action has an equal and opposite reaction. This is the two-beat of life. It is why when we exert or resist a great deal of energy without replenishing it, we later feel exhausted or burned out. For this reason, "to bring mind, body and spirit to peak condition, executives need to learn what world-class athletes already know: recovering energy is as important as expending it."[3]

Scott Barrett, the former chief information officer for a large public firm, described his experience as a younger manager this way:

"I remember a couple of situations where I reached the top of the curve and went over the other side. My manager, who could read me very well, said, 'Scott, you need to take a break. You need to take a four-day weekend. Don't take the phone with you. Don't take anything.' I wanted to stay with it but he was bright enough to see and say, 'You're leaving. Get your stuff; you are going home.'

"He didn't mean it in a negative way. Everybody wants to take on more than they probably should. Just as you need to learn to read people, you need to learn to read yourself. Most of us are probably not very good at it. We think we can take on more. I do think we need to walk away. And you need to maintain, from a health perspective, a balance of other things in your life, which I think will prevent you from hitting that pressure point and going off on the other side. Some people have been trained to take their phone and laptop with them and dial in to get their messages when they go on vacation. But you can't do that. You have to walk away from it. In most workplaces we are not dealing with life and death. We are trying to improve business, and we will be more productive if we not only treat people that way but treat ourselves that way."

Although it only takes minutes or seconds to re-center, we tell ourselves we are too busy, that we will do it later, or that the workplace doesn't support us in doing this. Oh yeah?

A couple of years ago, I participated in a jury selection for a retrial. The case was a serious one in which two men, who had been convicted of murder and were on death row, alleged that they were innocent and that they had been framed by the police. To protect potential jurors from information overload and potentially spacing out, the judge took movement breaks. Everyone including the lawyers, defendants, jury, bailiffs, press, and observers was ordered to stretch. The judge, herself, also stretched. When she first ordered everyone to rise and follow her movements, the attorneys were visibly shocked and the jury laughed, but we all rose, stretched to the ceiling, twisted our torsos, and wiggled our fingers. When she had to meet with the attorneys outside the courtroom, she would appoint someone to lead us in the stretches. People began to look forward to these breaks. The energy in the room became more alive as people got out of their heads and became centered and present.

⫸ PRACTICE: HOW TO CENTER

Step One: Pause

To change your mood and stress level, you first need to realize that you are no longer centered. This means that you need to stop and sense/feel inside you. Since you might forget to do this, here are a few suggestions you can use at work:

- Set your phone, clock, or timer to go off every sixty or ninety minutes. Stand up and sense/feel how you are.
- Create rituals in which the pause is built in so you can take time to assess your inner state. For example, every time you put the phone down or turn the computer on, pause before getting involved in the next task. Or, instead of rushing off to the next meeting, take a moment before you leave your office or cubicle to pause. Are you centered?
- Notice when someone or something grabs your attention. Initially, you may not be aware of it, but that person or object may be providing you with a clue to center/ground. Here are two examples:
  - Does the tall redwood tree you see from your office window capture your attention? It can serve as a reminder that there is an up and down energetic stream that moves through you. A

center. Better check to see if you are slouching or leaning towards one side of your body.

- Do you notice how surefooted the woman in the next office is? She moves so deliberately. Now notice how grounded you are. Can you even feel your feet?

Once you recognize the amazing intelligence of your attention, a tree will not only be a tree; it will be your wake-up call.

Step Two: Ways to Re-Center

Modern life has us paying attention to the future: our to-do lists, the next meeting, or upcoming deadlines. When your attention moves from center into what is in front of you, you lose a sense of your back, which supports you, and the ground that anchors you. To re-center yourself you need to get out of your head and shift your attention into your body. Here are some quick ways to shift your attention back to center:

- Take three deep breaths into your lower belly, allowing your rib cage and chest to expand wide rather than rise up.
- Take a walk, get something to eat, or speak to a colleague in person instead of writing an email. As you walk, feel the way your body moves. Experiment with moving with your attention in your *hara*.
- If your workplace has a campus in a natural setting, bring a blanket to work and lie on the ground. Spend five to ten minutes lying on your belly doing nothing and then flip over for another five to ten. You will be amazed at the energy you feel as your mood improves and your tension eases into the ground.
- Use humor to dispel the heaviness of your situation. Laugh your stress away by compassionately surrendering yourself to the imperfections, learning challenges, and moments of jerkiness that make us human.

- If your shoulders are tight sense/feel the soft angel wings that are connected to your shoulder blades. (Think John Travolta in the movie *Michael*.) As they expand wider than your physical body, feel the release of tension and your ability to sense your back increase.

- Once you have a sense of your back, it is easier to gain a sense of the ground. Imagine that you have a large, thick dragon tail growing from your lower back and resting comfortably on the ground. Notice how this helps drop your tension into the ground so you are moving with gravity instead of resisting it.

In the personal practice section you'll find a center/grounding exercise that I recommend you use daily. The more you engage in this practice, the more your muscles, tissues, and nerves will gain an intimate knowledge of center/ground. In time it will become second nature to recognize the difference between being centered from being off-centered, and easy to come back to a deeper and deeper home. After a while, as educator and author Peter Drucker suggests, you just may become a "master" of your energy.

PERSONAL PRACTICE

CENTERING PRACTICES

The following mind/body practice will show you how to center your-self quickly by mapping out what happens in your body as you leave and return to center. Approach these practices with the eye of a researcher. Pretend that you will be sharing with others what you learn about how we leave and return to center. After a while you will be able to re-center without going through all the steps and you may find your-self smiling.

Centering Practice

1. **Notice where you are.**
    a. Where is your attention? Is it outside of you in another person or situation, in your thoughts, or in your body?
    b. What do you notice in your body? Are certain muscles tight? Do you feel a particular emotion? If so, where?
    c. Without judgment, cartoon your posture by exaggerating how you are holding yourself together. For example, if your shoulders are high and tight, make them higher and tighter. If your chest is sunken in, let it sink even further. If your knees are locked, tighten them even more. This is your body's way of meeting the world. What are those raised shoulders, sunken chest, or locked knees saying? What is the way that you carry your body saying?

2. **Breathe deeply and slowly; sense/feel your tensions flow down into the ground.** Now imagine that there is a wide beam of light that ex-tends from over your head through your body and into the ground. We'll call this "center."

3. **Lean physically forward away from center and hold that position.** Ask yourself the following:
   a. What do you sense/feel in your physical body? Is your breath full or shallow?
   b. If you were to stand in this position for a long time, what might you feel emotionally?
   c. Is this position familiar to you? Does it have to do with future, past, or present?

4. **Let your body come back to center.**
   a. What happens in your body as you re-center?
   b. How does this place feel?
   c. How was your breath affected?
   d. How would you describe this place to someone who knows nothing about center?
   e. If you were standing here for a while, how would you feel emotionally? Does this place have to do with future, past, or present?

5. **Physically lean your body back** and ask the same set of questions you asked when you leaned forward.

6. **Let your body return to center** and again sense/feel into your body/energy field and notice what this level of center feels like.

7. **Energetically—not physically—lean forward.** Imagine that someone has something you want (e.g., the name of the person who will invest in your new app, the winning lottery numbers, or a proposal of marriage). Let your spirit reach out for it. Notice how your desire moves your physical body forward. If you were to function from this position for a long while, what might you sense and feel? How might you treat people? How would your performance be affected?

Some people like the experience of literally being on their toes. They feel closer to the action and more energized. For them, feeling calm is initially disconcerting. In doing this practice it doesn't matter what your preference is, just keep noticing what you sense/feel without judgment.

8. **Come back to center.** Describe how this experience of center differs from the other experiences in this practice. What is your relationship with the ground? Has it changed?

9. **Energetically—not physically—lean back.** Imagine there is something you want to avoid or that repels you (e.g., your boss chewing you out, an irritating coworker who wants to go to lunch with you). Your attention should be on the edge of your physical body or just behind it, not in your center. If you were to function from this position for a long while, what might you sense and feel? How would your performance be affected?

10. **Come back to center.** Describe how this experience of center differs from the other centering experiences in this practice. Now how would you describe yourself, your capacity, your confidence level, your integrity?

APPLICATION FOR TEAMS

WORK/LIFE INTEGRATION

"I don't think I can handle another five years at this pace," a vice president of human resources from the fashion industry told me. "I work ten- to twelve-hour days and take work home on the weekend." Her story is familiar. In previous decades, we thought a life lived from center meant dividing and balancing work and home in a prescribed way. Now, the multiple pressures of the workplace require a more spacious and flexible approach so that we can maintain our center and integrity while performing well on the job. Thus, today the balance between work and home life is more like a tide that ebbs and flows than a precise formula. It also varies for each individual. Therefore, savvy companies, compelled by the millennials, who think life is more than work, have replaced the work/life balance approach with an approach they call work/life integration.

At Novartis, Marcelo Fumasoni, vice president of human resources for Latin America and Canada, promotes awareness of this integration in a way that makes sense for the individual as well as the company. His intent is to provide consistency, not something that is dropped when a crisis occurs. Although there are global guidelines, Marcelo understands the nuances of each of his markets. Instead of insisting on strict regional policies, he supports a flexible approach in which markets can make decisions that serve them and their associates, thereby preserving their integrity. For example, a finance manager in Argentina is a competitive wind surfer. Since he can't accurately predict when conditions will be right for him to practice, the company supports his taking time off for his sport as long as it doesn't conflict with his work obligations. Another associate wanted to take a year off to explore ancestral medicine. Not wanting to lose him forever, the company let him follow his passion for a year. Marcelo, who travels frequently, models the same flexibility he offers others. While he is gone, his managers are empowered to make decisions regarding the day-to-day operations and only involve him on major decisions. When he returns, he'll take a long weekend to disconnect and recharge. This swing of attention from the professional to the personal and back again works well only when a company has a deep center/ground based on shared values and a respect for organizational and individual goals, which Novartis does.

Novartis also recognizes that it is difficult to create policies that address people's varied needs while creating a robust talent pipeline. Therefore, they encourage associates to discuss and negotiate work/life strategies with their managers. This flexibility and concern has earned Novartis the rank of one of the top twenty-five multinationals in the world.[4]

The best way to create work/life integration is to ask employees at all levels what they need to live a higher quality, more productive life. Create a band of ambassadors who take the pulse of the organization and collect suggestions. Or create world cafés that through inquiry reveal the collective wisdom of the group. However, no matter which way you gather, remember that the answers you seek come from the individuals and groups functioning from a deep center/ground. Guide them there and see what happens.

FIVE

WHEN THINGS ARE BAD, ENVISION YOUR BEST

Extending Your Energy for High Performance and Creativity

Miracles happen not in opposition to nature but in opposition to what we know about nature.

—Saint Augustine

n 1959, at the age of sixty-five, the Catalan poet and professor Pedro Bach-y-Rita had a massive stroke that paralyzed half his face and body, leaving him unable to talk or walk. After four weeks of rehabilitation therapy—the standard treatment at that time—Pedro showed little progress. Medical experts told his sons, George, a medical student who later became a psychiatrist, and Paul, a physician who became a neuroscientist and rehabilitation therapist, that Pedro should be institutionalized. Instead, George took him home with him to Mexico and personally provided therapy.

As George wasn't a rehabilitation expert, he had no set ideas about what was possible or impossible, which proved to be a godsend. He did know how babies learned, so he told his father, "You started off crawling, you will have to crawl again for a while."[1] Thus began a year's worth of instruction, until Pedro finally walked. Similarly, "mama" and "dada" eventually expanded to full speech competence. Pedro exercised around the clock by picking up coins with his dysfunctional hand, rolling marbles, washing pots, crawling in the garden, anything that might help him. After a number of months, he wanted to write. Again, he exercised, finger by finger, until he could once again type. By the end of only one year, he was almost completely recovered and returned to work full-time as a professor at City College in New York. A widower when he had the stroke, Pedro remarried and resumed hiking and traveling. At age seventy-two, while hiking at 9,000 feet in the mountains of Bogotá, Columbia, he had a heart attack and died shortly thereafter.

When asked in an interview why his father recovered from his stroke when so many others don't, George said his father trusted him and never got depressed. He believed he had a future, which motivated him.[2]

After Pedro died, an autopsy revealed that there was catastrophic damage to his brain stem; 97 percent of the nerves running from the cerebral cortex to the spine had been destroyed by the stroke. None of this damage had been repaired, yet Pedro had regained his physical capacities and led a normal life. Paul realized that through exercise his father's brain reorganized itself so that other parts could take over. Out of this potentially devastating experience, not only did Pedro regain a full life, but a new field of neuroscience, fathered by Paul Bach-y Rita, has enhanced the lives of countless others.

When things are bad, most people hunker down, contracting their energy or fighting desperately for control. The more they resist the pressure, which is there to help, the more they stifle their power, perceptions, and ability to navigate through their challenge. Seeing only the obstacles, their will weakens and they talk themselves out of their dreams and desires. That's what happened to Barry, a manager at a midsized technology company.

After eight years, Barry's job no longer challenges him, and his dislike of corporate politics has cooled his motivation for further advancement. Although he doesn't talk about his boredom, Barry spends hours on his Facebook page and daydreams about starting his own IT business. The idea excites him and his wife approves, yet he tells himself he can't because he has two children still in school and hasn't put enough money away for retirement. Whereas Barry believes he has no choice other than to tough it out, Pedro believed that the life he envisioned was possible. He therefore continued to exercise, and, as he did, his inner energy increased and he successfully achieved his desired vision.

THE POWER OF *KI* IN MEETING CHALLENGES

Energy, or *ki* flow, as it is known in Japan, is the fourth element of the inner map. It is the extension of *ki,* as it moves freely and harmoniously through our mind/body and out into the field around us, that maintains health, enlivens us, connects us with others, and provides a relaxed power and unique intelligence. *When concentrated in a single unified stream, this vital force can be channeled into a particular course of action or towards an objective or goal.* In fact, it is the quality, power, and direction of our *ki* flow that enable us to successfully navigate challenging situations.

However, *if the amount of energy coming at us is greater than the amount of energy/*ki *we project, we feel depleted, anxious, afraid, or stressed.* We may also feel intruded upon by other people's expectations or desires and be negatively affected by their comments or actions. When our energy outflow is low, our presence is contracted, and we may have difficulty influencing or persuading others to hear our point of view. However, when our *ki* is full and extended, we tend not to react negatively to others' judgments or criticisms. Instead of penetrating and harming us, they bounce off our energy field as an arrow bounces off a shield. *When our* ki *is extended, we feel confident, capable, and magnetic.* People notice us and listen more carefully to what we have to say.

In this chapter I'll identify the ways energy "speaks" to us so you'll know how to move with it instead of resisting it. We will also focus on how extending your energy positively affects your leadership presence and ability to attract what you want through visualization, and how it positions you to enter a flow state that produces high performance and creativity. For now, here's a quick way to enhance your energy.

THE YES . . . AND? TECHNIQUE

A few years ago, I worked with the senior research and development leadership team of a world-class beauty company, guiding them in creating a collaborative and emotionally intelligent culture for their division. Before each retreat, I interviewed each leader so I could design a program that would address their immediate concerns. On one occasion, I was surprised by their negativity. Sure, there were positive comments, but the negativity was weighing them down and limiting the amount of energy needed to unite them and move their division towards the next level of performance. Each was focused on their specific story; none recognized the damage their stories were doing.

In order to move forward, we had to confront the negativity. I designed two charts, which were covered when they entered the room. I unveiled the first one, an illustration of gray clouds crying. Beneath each cloud was a comment that I had collected from the interviews. They took turns reading the comments aloud. As they did, the energy of the room became constricted and dense. Halfway through the reading one participant said, "This is really a downer!" The others agreed. "Did we really say all this?" another asked. By the time they finished reading the comments, I knew the power of their collective negativity deeply affected them.

I then unveiled the second chart, an illustration of bright yellow sunflowers with their positive comments written under them. As they read them aloud, their spirits perked up and the energy in the room lightened. Laughing, they agreed that these comments felt better and acknowledged how easy it is to become stuck in an energy-depleting downward spiral. In fact, when we concentrate on our deficiencies, we strengthen them. Still, they did not want to pretend that things were okay when they weren't. The gift of the negative is that it tells us what isn't working. However, from "no" we have nowhere to go. That's when I offered them the Yes . . . AND? Technique.

"Yes" acknowledges what is, whether or not you like your current condition. It also doesn't mean that what is will go on forever. Physicists tell us that everything is in a state of constant movement and that life is continuously creating itself. However, when our minds become fixated on what we don't have or what we consider wrong, we impede this natural flow. The more we focus on the negative, the more anxious and stressed we become, particularly if we see no way out of our situation. Thus, the first step in regaining movement is to acknowledge what's bothering us.

There is something empowering about acknowledging aloud our concern; it dissipates some of its power when you give it a name and it becomes more manageable. The next step is to create an inquiry. The "AND" is a reminder that something else is also occurring. Maybe it is recognizing what's right in the picture, such as our capacity to see a bigger truth or a particular skill set we possess. Maybe it's a clue to how to solve the problem, a way of describing the situation that presents the problem in a new light. The AND creates energy movement through inquiry. *What's the next piece of information I need?* The AND implies, *what is going on that I'm not perceiving right now?* We don't need a big burst of inspiration, although that would be nice. All we truly need is a clue that opens the space a little and leads to the next clue. Just say "yes" to it or even "maybe" instead of an automatic "no"! Find the one clue that creates even the smallest movement and follow the energy. In time, the flow, which is intelligent, regains its inherent rhythm and intensity, and the problem will naturally unravel to reveal its secrets.

The Yes . . . AND? Technique resonated so much with the leaders of the R&D team that they rolled it out to the division. Instead of getting mired in the negative, they used the technique to propel them forward. Although the Yes . . . AND? Technique was a very small part of what made their culture shift, it helped create a mindset that supported success.

A Seed of Truth

"The longer we dwell on our misfortunes,
the greater is their power to harm us."
—VOLTAIRE

HOW ENERGY "SPEAKS" TO US

Think of energy as a friend who helps you perform and achieve your dreams. The key to mastery is learning to converse with energy, and to do that you need to understand its language.

Intent and Direction

Energy speaks of the movement of life. If we pay attention, it teaches us how to navigate and befriend it by continuously describing itself. When we sense/feel its movement, we discover that it has a purpose and path of its own. If we interfere with this flow by imposing our will, either we find that nothing we do moves us closer to our vision or goal or we are forcing the outcome and expending too much energy. This is the mechanical way of perceiving the world rather than an energy system approach. Though our ideas and plans may sound logical, even brilliant, this approach is draining and stressful and often causes more problems.

For example, years ago a neighbor complained that the vegetation in the lake had grown so tall that he no longer had a view of the water. The Homeowners' Association responded by removing all the vegetation. Problem solved—until the snakes that lost their home came on land. So they hired a company to remove the snakes. Problem solved—until the rats that lost one of their major food sources moved closer to the homes in search of food.

If we don't see life as an energetic system, we may not think past our first solution to see its ripple effect. If we step back, re-center, sense/ feel, and follow the energy movement, doors open and opportunities and solutions present themselves. Our new approach—the path of least resistance—feels effortless. When our intent and direction are in alignment, we are living our lives on purpose. In this state, force is replaced with effortless power.

Power and Intensity

From the gentle breeze to hurricane force winds, energy describes itself in terms of its level of power and intensity. We feel this power in the presence of great leaders and those whose hearts and integrity are strong. We know it in ourselves in those moments when doubts, fears, and self-consciousness fade away, and we stand full and present in the moment.

When energy speaks to us in terms of excitement, passion, or joy, most often we welcome and open to it. However, *if the intensity of the energy is more than we are comfortable with, we often back off and go in the opposite direction.* At times when I was younger, faced with something I said I wanted—a new consulting job, a great networking opportunity, a hot date—the closer the event, the more I didn't want to show up. My mind would spin stories: "I'm too tired," "I'll go next time," "He's not really what I want," and I'd miss opportunities to move my life forward. This is what happened to Barry, who dreamed of starting his own IT business, and what happens to so many of us.

Nadeau calls this the "180-degree turn." Once I learned how energy works, instead of being conned, I began opening to the energy. As my *ki* extends through energy practices, physical exercise, and/or shifting my thoughts, I feel excitement rather than dread. No longer do I feel prey to the energy; I am its welcoming committee. I've learned that when I dread doing something, I need to face it and do it, as there is usually some lesson or opportunity waiting for me. I also have learned that when the situation holds little energy, it doesn't matter whether or not I show up. BIG learning!

There are life events so huge that it's wise to take a moment to duck and catch your breath. Taking time to deal with the death of a loved one, think over the new promotion, or reconsider the job that partners you with a client you really don't like, is wise. It's all about choosing rather than reacting to the intensity of the energy and about learning to become as big as the energy wave that is pressing on you.

Energy Movement

Energy moves our lives in spirals, taking us up and down like the ocean's waves, as it spins into the unknown. Similarly, we see the spiral pattern reflected in the up and down movement of the stock market, the rise and fall of civilizations, and the birth, decline, and reinvention of product lines. Author William Bridges[3] talks about a spiral pattern in organizational and personal transitions. His work teaches us that the energy of change provides the momentum to move us from a lesser identity to an upgraded one. By sensing where we are within the spiral of transition and by opening and allowing the energy to flow freely through us, we are more equipped to surf the wave of change. We know that in time, the worst will be behind us and something new will take its place.

Often we fail to notice the spiral movement of energy in our own mind/bodies. In a meditation session for scientists, I asked participants to bring their awareness to any part of their body that felt constricted. As energy spirals from right to left and also from left to right, I asked them to find the spiral direction that tightened the body part and then to find the one that loosened it, and compared it to opening or closing the lid on a jar. The head of the department, who constantly felt tension in his back resulting from an old car accident, spoke first: "For the first time in years, I don't feel any pain."

Energy also describes itself in terms of length and width. There are days we feel small and want to be left alone and others when we feel tall and spacious. Feeling expanded naturally occurs when we are centered/grounded and our *ki* is extended. Although we may feel tall and large without being centered and grounded, the effects are different. Those experiences are idea- or ego-based, and may make us arrogant, elitist, or bullying. If we don't recognize where we are in terms of our alignment with energy, we may believe that our behavior is righteous, yet others intuitively recognize the difference even before we speak.

Energy also describes itself in terms of qualities and just as we have some choice in how we deal with the intensity, direction, intent, and movement of energy, we also have a say in the qualities we project and ultimately in our presence and character.

Qualities

As energy moves through us, it enriches us with qualities that make us the people we are. Since we are all part of the same energy field, each of us has all of the qualities, but in a unique mixture that distinguishes us. Looking back at your life, you will find that this mix shifts over time. At twenty, you may be easily angered by people's mistakes, but become more compassionate as you age. Perhaps you are kind, but later come to recognize that you can be kind as well as firm. If you live life well, aging upgrades your qualities, producing a positive shift in your character.

Similarly, you can upgrade who you are by dialoguing directly with energy. If you have deeply pondered a question, you know that in the quiet moment, an answer often appears. Eastern practices as well as the new physics recognize that the universe is responsive. However, most of us forget to ask. When I pose a question such as *what would it feel like if I was more patient, compassionate, or relaxed?* and am receptive and not judgmental, answers appear not only as ideas but as sensory experiences. Since success in any situation requires specific qualities, I also regularly ask for the qualities most necessary for a positive outcome when I facilitate a meeting, coach an executive, or work with a client. Through education and experience I have developed certain abilities, but like everyone else, I shine brighter and am more skilled on some days than on others. By dialoguing with energy, an upgraded Aimee, who I've come to trust, manifests. Other people sense these qualities in my presence, and like a "good" virus they, too, become "infected"; that is, they, too, are upgraded, which enables a new level of connection and interaction between us.

THE POWER OF PRESENCE

Even if you don't talk about energy at work, you sense the strength and quality of each other's *ki* flow. We call it their "presence." In the company of a U.S. president or top business leader, such as Bill Gates or Warren Buffett, we sense/feel their power. Watching Angelina Jolie on the red carpet, we not only see her beauty, grace, and power—which is very different from Warren Buffett's—we are touched and affected by it. Similarly, the Dalai Lama's presence evokes feelings of peace, happiness, and acceptance.

In business, as in life, what you project will either generate trust, connection, and support or repel others and create difficult, stressful situations. The more your energy extends, supported by a strong center/ground, the larger and more powerful your presence. However, if your *ki* is habitually low, you are not considered an important player.

Paul, an executive in a retail organization, shared this experience:

> "For a while I was on the fast track. I was promoted four times in two years. Then the promotions stopped. Four years went by and I couldn't figure out why I wasn't being promoted to vice president. I asked many people for feedback over those four years and not one could tell me why. Finally, one person said that when he saw me in the hallway, I never appeared to need to get somewhere."

Some people might take that feedback and begin rushing down the hallways, which wouldn't work. The feedback Paul received was really about how people experienced his presence, and shifting a person's presence requires a deeper approach.

Presence is the direct sensed/felt experience of *ki* or life energy as it flows and extends through you in the moment. Presence is not about arrogance or even charisma. Although its strength varies depending on your mood, health, and the situation, your presence always signals who you are.

Your unique presence reflects your inner qualities, level of consciousness, and how you think and feel about yourself. As authors Ron Kurtz and Dr. Hector Prestera state in their book *The Body Reveals,* "The reckless staggering of a drunk and the light graceful walk of a dancer speak as much to their movement through life as it does about how they move through space. It is as if the body sees what the mind believes, and the heart feels and adjusts itself accordingly."[4]

I asked a top executive, "What is the presence of a great leader?" He replied, "It is an air of confidence, not cockiness. It is a sense of humbleness, but not necessarily meekness."

Another leader told me, "It is the brightness or glow of a leader's confidence and inner strength. It is the projection of their belief in their self-worth." I asked her, "How do you see presence?" She replied, "Not with the eyes. You sense it in the way a person stands, the way the person holds herself. It is a strength that is more than the physical, which is projected through the body."

A few years ago, researchers from Columbia and Harvard discovered that a person's posture and presence affect their level of power.[5] People become more powerful, they found, when they assume an open, expansive pose by standing upright and spreading their arms and legs for a couple of minutes. Testosterone, the dominant hormone, increases, and cortisol, the stress hormone, decreases. This shift in hormones results in more confidence and a higher tolerance for risk that is reflected in the way they think and speak.

Although faking it by assuming this pose works, when faced with danger or conflict, it's hard to maintain. A more reliable method is learning to extend your *ki* flow through practice. (See the personal practice section of this chapter.) Practice imprints a neural pathway that enables

A Seed of Truth

*"Under duress we do not rise to our expectations,
we fall to our level of training."*

—BRUCE LEE

us to outflow our energy when under pressure, leading to confidence, joy, and power.

Researchers say that it takes 10,000 repetitions to imprint a new habit onto the nervous system. However, if you start small in situations that do not overwhelm you and then build up to more challenging ones, your leadership presence will grow and who you envision yourself to be will become who you are.

ENVISION YOUR BEST

In 1978, Shakti Gawain's book *Creative Visualization: Use the Power of Your Imagination to Create What You Want in Your Life* was published. Before I knew it, the Oakland As and the Giants were using visualization as a means to higher performance. I blinked twice and corporations were writing vision statements and nailing them on the wall. Similarly, entrepreneurs, dreamers, and success chasers in every occupation became smitten with the idea that if they could envision it, it was possible. For many, visualization became part of their meditations, and affirmations were elevated to the status of prayer. Today visualization, once considered woo-woo, is mainstream. Although some prosper through visualization, others flail or fail.

Visualization—a mind/body/energy experience—begins with an intention or desirable image that you project onto the larger electromagnetic field. As your intention is composed of energy, it has direction, intensity, and qualities. The more you sense/feel the qualities of your image and the stronger you project it, the more the image imprints a magnetic track that attracts what you want. The more precise and focused your intention, the more power it has. Thus, it's important not to have conflicting beliefs about what you desire. For a visualization to be most potent, it needs the sharp focus of a surgeon. Most of us have not honed that skill or eliminated conflicting beliefs. Yet, if your desire is just somewhat stronger than your conflict, you will see movement and progress.

Sometimes, the strength of your desire can initially override your conflicting belief. My friend Frank was an exceptional entrepreneur who learned as an army ranger in Vietnam how to focus and extend his energy in order to survive. He used this skill in his business and became a millionaire. A couple of years later, he was broke. He told me there was a part of him that didn't believe he deserved the wealth. *To achieve and maintain your vision, you must be as energetically big and vibrating as finely as that which you desire.* Conflicting beliefs will always limit the intensity of your energy outflow particularly over time. In Chapter 6, we'll look at how your energetic size makes a difference in handling life's challenges and how you can increase it.

In the meantime, it's important to recognize the wisdom in life's timing. We get what we are ready for: what we are big enough and capable enough to handle. Think about the people who got what they said they wanted—performers, athletes, lottery winners, and, yes, the guy in the next cubicle who so desperately desired that promotion, only to have it stress and/or devastate them. In the lowest of lows, it helps to remind yourself that you have been provided with enough, that you are still here, and the show is not over. Instead of bemoaning your fate, it's time to practice and refine not only your skills, but your relationship with yourself and the electromagnetic field that nurtures and sustains you.

Similarly, in the highest of highs, life is not only a joy and celebration of success, it's an opportunity to experience and remember on a neural level what extended energy supported by a deep center and ground feels like. Once you habitually embody this way of being, things become ex-

A Seed of Truth

"Everything is energy and that's all there is to it. Match the frequency of the energy and you cannot help but get that reality. It can be no other way."

—ALBERT EINSTEIN

tremely interesting. No longer is life about fighting pressure; it's about opening to pressure and allowing it to enhance performance and the quality of life by living in the moment. And if you are lucky, you experience the flow or what athletes call "being in the zone."

LETTING GO: THE FLOW STATE

I am at the annual aikido retreat getting ready to sing "The Rose" during talent night. I've practiced this song many times and truly love it. As I wait for the MC to call my name, I feel so juiced my heart is racing. This is a good thing; the increased energy will enhance my performance. I breathe, open to center/ground, and surrender to the energy. The music starts and I begin to sing. My concentration is deep and focused, but it is not located in my thinking mind. Instead, every cell in my body is alert and activated.

Almost immediately, I realize the song sounds different from when I practiced it. I have the words, rhythm, and melody right, but the nuances, the phrasing, the feeling, are all new. I recognize that I am out of control and am a bit scared. I can't call a do over, so I let go and surrender to it. When the song ends, my teacher, Robert Nadeau, runs onto the stage, picks me up, and hugs me. The energy feels so big I am elated. Later, I realize I had entered a flow state, and that Bob, a master of energy, had witnessed it and was delighted for me.

According to Professor Mihaly Csikszentmihalyi, "Flow denotes the holistic sensation present when we act with total involvement."[6] Although people talk about being lost in their thoughts, the flow state Csikszentmihalyi describes is a full mind/body/energy experience in which our thinking mind is quieted so the body's intelligence can take over and do what it instinctively knows to do and/or was trained to do. Action and awareness are merged without regard to results or control. In this state, we are relaxed while experiencing a heightened level of mastery that has an efficiency of energy.

All of us have had these moments—on the sports field, while making love, or at work. While in the flow, we become more creative and intuitive, gaining access to information we do not usually have. Bill Russell describes this experience in his autobiography, *Second Wind: The Memoirs of an Opinionated Man*:

> At that special level, all sorts of odd things happened. . . . It was almost as if we were playing in slow motion. During those spells, I could almost sense how the next play would develop and where the next shot would be taken. Even before the other team brought the ball in bounds, I could feel it so keenly that I'd want to shout to my teammates, "It's coming there!"—except that I knew everything would change if I did. My premonitions would be consistently correct, and I always felt then that I not only knew all the Celtics by heart but also all the opposing players, and that they all knew me.[7]

Entering the Flow

Can you imagine what life would be like if instead of being stuck in the small, repetitive thinking of our minds, our focus on the past or future, and our knee-jerk reactions to energy, we let go and were present in the flow of life as it manifests each moment? Now imagine what it would be like if those we worked with joined us in this state. Most of us have been there. It's those extraordinary meetings when we collectively are in such an elevated flow that ideas keep popping, and we walk away from the meeting feeling energized. Instead of just forgetting about it, we go home and share what happened with our loved ones. Who wouldn't say, "Give me more of that!"? Although we can't push ourselves into the flow, we can put ourselves at its doorway by becoming truly familiar with this state through practice rather than waiting for inspiration.

It is helpful to recognize that flow and structure are partner energies. Flow without structure leads to chaos. Structure without flow is boring and leads to limiting habits and business as usual. Over time, as the flow builds it will outgrow the structure and transform it.

Although you do not have to be a master, the experienced practitioner is more likely to enter the flow state than the beginner. Practice imprints efficient neural pathways and develops muscle memory that is essential to skillful action. The flow state is more available when you open to center/ground and your energy outflow merges with the larger electromagnetic field. Thus, the inner map detailed in these chapters (attention, center, ground, *ki* flow) is the foundation not only for preventing and relieving stress, but also for higher functioning. When you combine this basic internal map with an intention, you are ringing the doorbell of the flow state. If you are lucky enough for the door to open, staying in the flow requires letting go of control and moment-by-moment full sensory attention on the present. Then all you need is enough inner space to handle the intensity of the energy flow so you don't freak out and resist it. In Chapter 6, I'll show you how to enhance your capacity.

For now, focus on keeping your energy outflow strong and take care of replenishing it regularly. You'll not only feel more confident and passionate about your work, but in time, others will feel your fire and spread it. Soon a ripple effect will occur. Eventually the energy will build to the point where it blows out everything that was limiting you. Will you then end up a millionaire or the CEO of your company? Maybe or maybe not.

However, when you live and work with an embodied gusto, you are more likely to attract meaningful opportunities and the right people to you. You'll feel a satisfaction and inner joy that no amount of money can buy. And in the darkest of times, like Pedro Bach-y-Rita after his stroke, you'll know there is a future.

PERSONAL PRACTICE

DEVELOP YOUR *KI*/ENERGY OUTFLOW

Mind/Body Practice: The Unbendable Arm

One of the basic practices in aikido for demonstrating and developing *ki* is called the unbendable arm. Here's how you practice it.

Extend your arm in front of you with your fingers outstretched. As you sense/feel the energy move out through your fingers, the flow will become more intense and your fingers will seem longer. Now relax your muscles and sense/feel your palm and the underside of your arm; allow it to feel supported as if it was resting on a ledge. Continue to concentrate on a point beyond your extended fingertips. You may want to project the stream onto the wall in front of you, which will lengthen the flow.

Next, practice extending *ki* through your other arm. Then practice lifting both arms at the same time, imagining, for example, that your arms and hands are headlight beams. Notice that the energetic field or circle around you begins to expand as your *ki* extends and that your mood improves. If you do not sense/feel anything or the energy seems to be stuck, try the Yes . . . AND? Technique. The slightest sensation will lead to another.

Last, ask someone to try to bend your arm by pressing down on it just above the elbow. If you allow the flow of energy to move out beyond your fingertips and do not resist or tense your muscles, your partner will be unable to bend your arm.

Reflective Practice

What is your vision of thriving at work? What does it look like and feel like? Who would you be if you were thriving? What type of projects would you be doing? How would you respond to pressure or challenges? How would people treat you? How would you treat others? To clarify your vision, write down your answers to these questions. Then ask yourself:

- Did I dare dream big enough?
- Is my vision achievable and measurable? What criteria would I use to measure it?
- Is my vision good for all concerned?
- What do I need to give up in order to achieve my vision?
- Do I have the level of consciousness and sense of self that is necessary to achieve this vision? If not, in what ways do I need to grow?
- Who would I define myself as if I attain this vision?

Once you know what you want, sit quietly with your eyes closed and take a few deep breaths into your lower belly, relax, and open to center/ground. Once you feel embodied and expanded, sense/feel your vision. Be aware of the details of your visualization—how far your presence is extended, what you are wearing, the qualities you project, etc.

APPLICATION FOR TEAMS

Increasing Positive Energy in a Work Environment

Vishen Lakhiani is the founder and CEO of Mindvalley, a small personal development company in Malaysia that is doing big things. His leading edge organizational processes are transforming his business culture to make it more effective. Vishen understands that when the energy is flowing in a positive manner, the workplace takes on a vibrancy that enhances productivity, employee engagement, and bottom line results. He recognizes that combined with a visioning process, this formula generates happy employees with big dreams—a potent combination. Mindvalley has installed some practices and rituals that keep the energy pumping, employees highly engaged, and the revenues rising. Some of these might work for your team and/or organization.

Daily Gratitude Log

Mindvalley believes that what you appreciate appreciates. Therefore, it created a company gratitude website. Employees, family members, customers, and partners are invited to post entries about whatever they are grateful for that has occurred over the last twenty-four hours. The thinking behind this is that by acknowledging what you are grateful for, you maximize your happiness and grow those parts of your life. It also provides Vishen an opportunity to learn what is making his community happy.

Awesomeness Report

Instead of traditional company meetings in which people focus on what went wrong, everyone meets weekly to celebrate what went right and to recognize that week's outstanding employees. The intent is to increase employee happiness by formalizing the gratitude process.

A day before the meeting, employees send Vishen a weekly update that includes things they did outside of work; sales records that they broke; innovations, new product launches, etc., that they consider awesome. These are compiled into a motivating PowerPoint that celebrates their successes.

Profit Sharing

Every month 10 percent of the profits go to employees. By tying the company's revenue goals to employees' goals, they create alignment, and employees are willing to put in extra time when needed.

Group Guided Meditation/Visioning

Every week the staff gathers to engage in a guided meditation in which they visualize their life in six to twelve months including such things as what their work will look like, how big their bonus check will be, what their personal life will be like, what promotion they will receive, and so on.

Cosponsored Fun

Mindvalley is known for its great parties. Because they believe people are more engaged and productive when they have friends at work, they create experiences in which employees can bond. Some of these parties also serve as a recruitment method; employees are asked to bring their two smartest friends.

Positive Stamina

When things go wrong at Mindvalley—the server goes down, someone made a big mistake—instead of concentrating on what went wrong, employees make vision boards showing where they want their project to be. In most cases, by focusing on their vision, they come up with solutions that make the problem irrelevant.

Talent Development

To groom people, Vishen exposes his staff to brilliant minds. He hosts parties at which the speakers mingle with his employees. He also sends employees to conferences around the world and encourages friendships between his employees and his clients, many of whom are authors. By exposing them to thought leaders, they develop professionally, their confidence rises, and their presence expands.

SPLASH (Secret Society of Platonic Love, Appreciation, Smile, and Happiness)

This is an undercover department at Mindvalley and nobody knows who is in it.

When people become too stressed, their job is to do something outrageous that will relieve the tension.

SIX

SIZE MATTERS

Becoming as Big as the Job

I've suffered a good many catastrophes in my life. Most of them never happened.

—Mark Twain

The other day, I woke up brimming with energy and a sense of well-being. My body felt relaxed and my presence seemed to fill the room. Inspired, I sat down to write an article about my aikido experience, which had been commissioned for an anthology. The words came through so effortlessly it was almost as if it wrote itself. Sensing I was on a roll, I called Chuck, the learning and development manager of a pharmaceutical company, and spoke with him about a potential coaching assignment. My passionate explanation of my coaching approach wowed him. I hung up knowing that I had made his shortlist and potentially found an ally. Soon after, I heard from Diana, who was setting up a customer service center for a world-class beauty company. Somehow, I knew exactly what to say. When our conversation ended, she was convinced that I was the right consultant for the job.

All afternoon the phone buzzed with new connections and possible jobs. Confidently, I decided to take on the Veteran's Administration, who had erroneously lowered my mom's monthly benefit. It was a piece of cake. The VA representative saw the error and agreed to submit new paperwork. I felt happy, empowered, and as big as every job I took on.

The next day, I had a bad case of the blahs. I felt tense, small, and disconnected from myself. Not wanting to succumb to the feeling, I started working on changes to my book proposal suggested by my agent. No matter how long I stared at the screen, I was unable to find the words. I gave up and decided to focus on completing tasks I'd been postponing. First, I called a couple of potential clients but neither was available. Next, I called the phone company to ask about their bundles, hit the wrong button, and waited ten minutes only to be connected to the wrong department. Finally, I was transferred, and was once again on hold. Annoyed after another ten minutes, I hung up. Next, I called my kind and patient tech consultant, who said he would take care of my problem, but an hour later, he hadn't solved it. Normally, I would shrug it off; that day I was impatient and judgmental.

The rest of the day was no better. By the end of the day, my emotions were so raw that if anyone had made any demand on me, I knew I'd end up crying or yelling. I told myself I was just having a bad day, but I didn't really understand why. Nothing external had changed.

Although most of us live our lives somewhere between these two extremes, the quick shift from one experience of ourselves to another should be familiar to most readers. With every change in the size of our mind/body/energy field, we see the world differently and must learn to work with the opportunities and challenges that these changes pose. Although we may not be able to control external events, we do have the ability to choose how we interpret them.

YOUR STATE OF MIND VS. REALITY

An old farmer had an old horse for tilling his fields. One day the horse escaped into the hills. When his neighbors sympathized with him over his bad luck, he replied, "Bad luck? Good luck? Who knows?"

A week later the horse returned with a herd of wild horses; this time the neighbors congratulated him on his good luck. His reply, "Good luck? Bad luck? Who knows?"

When the farmer's son attempted to tame one of the wild horses, he fell and broke his leg. Everyone commiserated over this very bad luck. Not the farmer. He responded, "Good luck? Bad luck? Who knows?"

Some weeks later, the army marched into the village and conscripted every able-bodied youth. When they saw his broken leg, they let the son off. Was that good luck? Bad luck? Who knows?

None can say; reality is subjective. Your state of mind determines what you perceive and think, how you interpret your experiences, and what you draw to you. Your state of mind is at the center of what I call a "version of yourself," and your behavior is a natural expression of it.

The Many Versions of You

Each of us has many versions of ourselves; they operate on a continuum from lower to higher consciousness. The higher your consciousness, the more you operate from your purest self and the more connected you feel to others and the living system in which you live. When consciousness fluctuates, we call this a shift in our mood or state of mind. The lower your consciousness or mood, the more negative your view of life and the more isolated you feel. In lower versions of self, we are reactive, creating tension in ourselves and friction with others. This state of mind is often accompanied by feelings of depression, fear, or anger. However, the higher your state of consciousness is, the greater your capacity and ability to function and relate. In more spacious versions of ourselves, we feel confident, creative, happy, and powerful. My teacher, Robert Nadeau, describes this continuum using the many versions of him as an example. He calls these versions Bobby, Bob, Robert, Mr. Nadeau, and Sensei Nadeau. Bobby is the kind of guy who might get sand thrown in his face at the beach. He takes up very little space, has a difficult time articulating what's on his mind, and seems to want to be left alone. Women want to mother him and men pass him by. With each upgrade, Bob's presence expands and he becomes bigger and more powerful. At the level of Sensei he possesses the lethal ability of a samurai, expresses himself exactly, has the multiperceptual ability to map out internal states of consciousness, and intuitively knows how to work with students to enhance their abilities. As Sensei Nadeau, illustrated in Figure 6-1, women want to do more than mother him and men stand up and take notice.

Similarly, at each upgraded version of you, your perceptions, wisdom, ability to deal with pressure, and skill in action are enhanced. A review of the stellar moments of your life as well as its nadirs will affirm that size matters!

IIII▶PRACTICE: To help you with this, do the following exercise and then see Table 6-1 for the same exercise completed by a radio personality and author.

1. Name three versions of yourself: the small one, the average one—the one you usually operate from, and the largest one. The names should reflect the identity. Write them down. Have fun with this. For example, Beyoncé calls her courageous and sexy stage persona Sasha Fierce in contrast to the smaller, generally shy, version of herself. Having stepped into Sasha Fierce's shoes for so many years, Beyoncé no longer needs Sasha Fierce, because she's now able to merge the two.

2. In the next row, write down the physical manifestation of each of the versions. For example, round-shouldered, shallow breathing or breathing in my lower belly, move from my hips, very grounded, feel contracted or expanded, and so on.

Figure 6-1. Sensei Nadeau demonstrating "outflow" to his students.
PHOTO BY VERA SMIRNOVA

3. Next, write down the qualities and emotions of each identity. Notice how these shift, as you become your next bigger version, for example, from rigid and anxious to fluid and confident, and so on.

A Seed of Truth

"If you are distressed by anything external, the pain is not due to the thing itself but to your own estimate of it; and this you have the power to revoke at any moment."

—MARCUS AURELIUS

4. List the most prevalent thoughts and actions each version of you has, for example, negative or positive thoughts; moves against, away, or towards others; blames self or others; and so on. Does each version of you have different feelings about you and others?

5. Last, write down what each identity attracts most easily to itself such as negative people, smiles, information, help, money, and so on.

Table 6-1. Three versions of a radio personality.

NAME OF IDENTITY	ISABEL	TOOTSIE	GLINDA
Physical Experience	Shallow breathing; contracted; tightness in stomach and solar plexus; feels small	More room than Isabel has, yet still feels contracted; energetically leaning forward; left and right sides unequal	More room to move around in; stronger in stance; feels supported; has a sense of her back; feels aligned
Qualities and Emotions	Competitive; jealous; feels unworthy; lacks confidence	Defiant, fearful; feels threatened	Happy; confident, empowered

Thoughts and Actions	Negative inner dialogue; self-deprecating; talks herself out of taking risks	Acts the joker; minimizes the process; mumbles under breath; sarcastic	Authentic sense of self; guidance comes from inner self; able to process clearly, able to transform self; empowers others
What It Attracts	Criticism; emotional neglect; financial struggle; career opportunities pass her by	Attention; arguments; drama; insensitivity to her softer side; begins to attract career opportunities	Career and financial opportunities and success; attention; kindness, admiration, recognition

SHIFT GEARS: FIND A NEW PERSPECTIVE

Janet, as I'll call her, a senior city attorney, disagreed with one of her colleagues. Neither woman was willing to consider the other's point of view. Instead, each shifted into a smaller version of herself. Janet said, "We were like two little kids." That weekend, Janet was preoccupied with what she wanted to say to her coworker, clever ways to demean her, and how to defend her own point of view. By Monday, she had shifted her state of mind. Her colleague had maintained her smaller identity and the attendant hostility. Instead of re-engaging after a verbal barb, Janet shifted to an even larger version of her, and did not respond. Her coworker intuitively sensed the deep shift in Janet and her own hostility melted. The tension was released, and the dispute was over. They were then able to resolve the problem.

Psychologists call this process of observing in a new light or approaching a challenge from a different perspective "cognitive reframing." "Getting fired," one executive told me after his initial reaction of fear and rejection subsided, "was the best thing that happened to me. It propelled me to pursue my dream of starting my own business." " I was so stressed from being micromanaged," another man shared, "that I developed diverticulitis. I was ready to quit until my wife asked me if I had discussed my concerns with my boss. I realized that, although I had many reasons not to share my perspective, the truth was that communicating how I felt was difficult for me. This experience significantly changed my life. Had it not been for the fear I felt being in so much physical pain, I don't think I would have been inspired to develop communication skills." Cognitive reframing is about seeing the good in what we initially perceive as bad, the larger picture in what first seems limiting.

Move Up: Free Yourself from Your Triggers

To move into a larger version of self requires easing away from the ego-driven personality in order to welcome the deeper levels of who you are. The more you recognize the triggers that position you to fight or flight, the more able you are to revoke their license over you and evolve. See Table 6-2 for the specific causes of each Enneagram type's stress and anger.[1]

Table 6-2. Causes of stress and anger according to the Enneagram.

	STRESS TRIGGER	ANGER TRIGGER
Type 1. The Perfectionist	Thinking I am not good enough When everything seems to be my responsibility Too many mistakes to correct	People who break the rules or are irresponsible Unjust criticism
Type 2. The Giver	Emotional upheaval in relationships Too many people and projects rely on me Not being sure of what I need	Feeling unappreciated or undervalued Feeling controlled Unmet personal needs

Type 3. The Performer	Equating my worth with my accomplishments, status, or power Not knowing my real feelings or worth Too much to do	Anything or anyone that stands in the way of my success Incompetence Indecisiveness
Type 4. The Romantic	When people and things don't meet my idealized expectations Envy Unmanageable feelings	People who abandon or let me down Feeling misunderstood Phoniness
Type 5. The Observer	Insufficient boundaries and privacy Fatigue Depending on others for what I want	Accusations of being factually incorrect Demands and intrusions Emotional overload
Type 6. The Trooper	Uncertainty and insecurity Difficulties with authority figures Trying to maintain the goodwill of those I don't really trust	Betrayal Feeling cornered, pressured, or controlled by others When people don't respond to me
Type 7. The Epicure	Trying to experience all options Repeating my mistakes Making commitments and then feeling trapped by them	Limits that prevent me from getting what I want People who are unhappy and stuck and those who blame others
Type 8. The Boss	Inability to correct injustices Containing my confrontational style Denying the pain and fatigue that come from overdoing	Deceit, manipulation People who won't stand up for themselves Attempts to control me

Type 9. The Mediator	Having to make timely decisions and set priorities Having someone angry at me because I said "No" Having to live up to a commitment I didn't want to make	Being treated as unimportant Feeling controlled by others Being forced to face conflict

Though each personality type has specific triggers, whether we become stressed and/or angry and the level of intensity is not the same for all members of that type. This is determined by the level of consciousness from which you operate. For example, Type 8s (e.g., Dr. Phil) tend to have easy access to their life energy. Their anger is readily available and they have an energetic way of owning the room that is apparent to others. In the smallest unhealthy version of Type 8s (e.g., Saddam Hussein), under pressure, they may use their energy to destroy others rather than let them win or gain control. Having little tolerance for diverse opinions, they can become destructive, terrorizing, and ruthlessly dictatorial.

In more average versions, when under pressure, Type 8s may be confrontational, intimidating, dismissive, and guard their feelings. They may be bullying. As their level of consciousness increases, they begin to serve the greater good rather than their own ego needs like Lyndon Baines Johnson.

Larger versions of Type 8 tend to be protective of others without being controlling, thus bringing out the best in people. As they let down their guard, their large hearts open, and they lead through love rather than fear.

Characteristics of the Smaller Self

A brilliant scientist, Andrea has innovated products that have contributed significantly to the organization's bottom line. Andrea is a highly creative, deep thinker with a long-range view. She is attracted to the unique and disdains the mundane. She sees herself as special and claims people don't understand her. In conversation, she rarely looks people in the eye and tends either to entertain or one-up people; that doesn't leave much room for a true connection. Yet, Andrea expects others to trust her point of view.

When the economy plummeted, Andrea took a job for which she was overqualified; this demotion hurt her pride. Although she pitched ideas for new products to the marketing department, they rejected them. Now in her late fifties, Andrea wonders if she has lost her edge. Instead of focusing on expanding her creativity and/or improving her ability to communicate and influence, she shifts to her smaller self and assumes a victim role, claiming that she has no power and that at her age, she can't do anything to change things.

The smaller self always tells a limiting story. Yet, for as much as the smaller self complains about its circumstances, it refuses to budge from its perspective. In fact, the more the smaller self tells its tale, the more extreme the story becomes and the more it believes it is true.

A recovering alcoholic told me the following classic AA story:

Joseph wakes up one morning twenty minutes later than usual. When he realizes the time, he becomes agitated thinking that he will be late for work. He tells himself, "The boss is going to be really mad. I was late three months ago. There goes my promotion. I worked so hard for that promotion. He could fire me. He hates when people are late. No question about it, I'm going to lose my job. If I lose my job, the bank will foreclose on the house. We'll have nowhere to live. My wife is going to be furious with me. She'll leave me. She'll take the kids and move to her mother's. I'll only get to see the kids a couple of weeks a year." In less than five minutes, Joseph had gone from being twenty minutes late for work to having his whole life crash in on him. The smaller self is like that. It weaves negative stories that it believes and defends, and is hurt or angry when others don't see it that way.

Intimate knowledge of the smaller versions of ourselves may influence us to believe we are damaged or flawed, but we are not flawed. The smaller self is perfect as the smaller self. It is senseless to try to argue, coerce, educate, or cure the smaller self; it's not going to change. The inner child will never grow up. Little Bobby will never be Sensei Nadeau. Neither will the smaller self die. It will be there throughout your life. Although you may not normally operate from your smaller self, if the pressure is great enough, you may revisit that smaller version of you.

Tanika, the CEO of a nonprofit organization serving the homeless, is respected locally and nationally for her fearlessness in taking on difficult challenges as well as her willingness to share control, visibility, and credit. She speaks with an open heart and gives people the benefit of the doubt. She is a strategic innovator, successfully guiding her organization through difficult economic times. People trust Tanika.

For the last eight years, Tanika's COO has been Linda, an experienced therapist and operations leader. The women generally work well together and deeply care for each other. They also set off one another's trigger. When Linda senses inequality or thinks she has been left out of the communication loop, she reverts to the little girl who had to fight for her fair share. Instead of talking with Tanika as an ally, she becomes highly emotional and makes judgmental and blaming accusations.

Tanika maintains her presence throughout these confrontations, but feels frustrated, misunderstood, and resentful. Recently, the board reimbursed Tanika for damages done to her minivan in the organization's parking lot, but, since there was no policy in place, they decided to create a new policy exempting it from future liabilities. Tanika feared Linda would see this as an unfair entitlement and turn it into a protracted conflict, and so did not notify Linda immediately. Tanika shifted to the smaller version of herself that feared being vulnerable and inadequate. Thus, this usually strong, principled, and very competent woman chose to avoid.

Reprogram Yourself: Change Channels

Making the shift into a larger version of yourself tunes you in to a different type of mental programming. Think of it this way: If you did not have premium cable access, you might not know HBO existed. You'd exist on a diet of situation comedies, police dramas, reality programs, soaps, and daytime talk shows. Your view of what television had to offer would be quite limited. Similarly, through habit, your mind is attached to specific channels or energy frequencies. To expand your view and experience of reality, you must tune in to other frequencies that are available when you are more open. By shifting channels or frequencies, you shift your level of consciousness and your state of mind.

All of us, however, have had moments when a limited or negative voice has held us captive. In those moments, cut the flow of the thought pattern by shifting your attention. Say to yourself, "Cancel," and imagine you are changing channels. Come back to the here and now and sense/feel your presence. If you are being held hostage by distressing thoughts, distract yourself by remembering your last vacation, an exciting upcoming work project, your amazing golf shot, or any other happy thought.

However, for reframing to be successful, it must be more than replacing a negative thought with a positive one, which only works if your attachment to the negative belief is not too strong. If you merely swing from one thought to its opposite, you'll often swing back to where you started. To shift to a higher level of consciousness and avoid mental flip-flopping, you must expand the process of reframing from the cognitive alone to encompass the mind/body/energy field.

Reframing in the mind/body/spirit realm is like opening the door to allow fresh air into the house. It wakes you and sharpens your perceptions. If you step outside, you see what lies beyond your fear. Moreover, you sense/feel the depth of the ground and the vastness of the sky, you have more space to move in, and, therefore, feel freer and more empowered to handle your issue. You become as big as the job. Instead of resisting the pressure, whole system reframing helps you see the opportunities inherent in the situation. You not only think about things differently, your body relaxes and your spirits lift. In time, you realize that you are limited only by your mind. As your energy field is part of an infinite field, there are no boundaries to who you are. (In the personal practice section, I will show you how to take more space and upgrade your identity.)

Some people call shifting to a larger version "taking the high road." I remind them that it is not only high; it is deep and wide. The larger version has an expanded presence that expresses itself authentically. People may not be cognitively aware of it, but they sense it in others. They will either be uplifted by another person's higher consciousness or, if they choose to hold onto the smaller versions of themselves, disturbed by it. Therefore, great leaders such as Martin Luther King, John Kennedy, and Gandhi are followed and loved as well as feared.

Big in One Aspect, Small in Another

Excellence in any endeavor requires a spaciousness that results from an openness and alignment with the larger energy field. Yet, operating from your larger version in one area of your life in which you excel doesn't necessarily mean that you are that large in every other aspect of your life.

The athlete with all the right moves on the field may make all the wrong moves in business. However, it's not just athletes; think about all the prominent people who were duped by Bernie Madoff. Similarly, the in-control businesswoman may be a pushover when it comes to her kids. The extraordinary coach may be a fabulous strategist on the field, but unable to make strategic decisions in his everyday life. The shy woman who never speaks up at meetings may be a killer on the tennis court.

Executives who assume that excellence automatically translates from one aspect of their life to another may be operating more from ego than from fact. For example, the CEO of a technology company asked Andrew, her training director, to develop a course that would help employees understand and operate from the company's values of collaboration, trust, innovation, diversity, courage, and community citizenship. Beginning at the bottom of the corporate ladder, Andrew worked his way up and got rave reviews from the front line and managers alike.

As each level went through the program, the organization's culture incrementally changed for the better. As trust grew, more people spoke their minds instead of deferring to the loudest speaker. This diversity of thinking led to better collaboration as more people became engaged. Their focus on corporate community citizenship inspired them to consider the greater good of the whole company rather than the interests of their silos or only themselves. Although most were cautious about this change, increased innovation emerged as accountability and commitment grew. Excited, many associates and mid-level managers asked Andrew when senior leaders would attend the program. Some executives acted like patriarchs, played favorites, and, in some cases, distrusted other executives. Senior managers tended to collude with a code of silence rather than speak their minds and work out their differences. "How can we embrace these values fully if our bosses do not?" many associates complained.

When Andrew approached Roberta about scheduling a time for her and her direct reports to go through the program, she objected. "We developed these values. Why waste our time reviewing them?" Ultimately, Andrew threw up his hands and gradually ended the training effort. Without executive role models, people soon sank back to their old ways.

In this case, the CEO's arrogance prevented her from seeing she was locked in a smaller version of herself. It can happen to any of us. If we are lucky, someone we are willing to listen to puts a mirror right in front of us. "Leave your ego at the door," a wife demanded of her brilliant and successful attorney husband. "This house is not big enough for the three of us." Panicked that she might leave, he began to change. A year later, I saw them at a retreat. He looked more relaxed and less rigid, and told

A Seed of Truth

"We are the one common factor in all we perceive
and do. As we change ourselves, our entire world
changes and is made new."

—STEPHEN SAMUELS

me that he had fewer turnovers in his office, his business was booming, and his relationship with his wife was great. His misunderstanding, he said, was in thinking that he was entitled to his "do it my way or the highway" attitude. He realized that his arrogance was a cover-up for his smaller self's fear of inadequacy. This discovery led him to find a way to shift to a larger, more authentic version of himself. As a result, his attitudes and behaviors changed.

PERSONAL PRACTICE

SHIFT TO A LARGER VERSION OF YOURSELF

All of us have ways that help us shift our state of mind. Some of the more common approaches include being in nature, exercise or sports of any kind, deep breathing, meditation, and laughing or other type of emotional catharsis. However, the workplace does not usually allow us the time for many of these methods. Still, we often need to shift our state of mind quickly during our workday. The following, if practiced, will imprint new neural pathways, which will allow you to respond in empowering ways.

Mind/Body/Energy Practice

When I have an important meeting or phone call scheduled, I prepare by shifting to a larger version of me to enhance my performance. The following practice takes only five to ten minutes once you get used to it. Just trust whatever you feel and sense. I've included the responses of Jeff, a coaching client, to enhance your understanding of the process.

Instructions: While standing with legs comfortably apart, lean down and touch the floor. Imagine all your tensions and thoughts being released into the ground. When you are ready, ask yourself, *what would it be like to be 10 percent more here*? This is a rhetorical question and does not need a cognitive response, but, as you stand up, let your hands sense/feel the energetic circle that starts at the ground, widens around you, and flows over your head. Take a moment to notice the state of your mind/body field.

Jeff: "I take a deep breath and notice my feet on the floor. A minute ago, I knew I had feet, but I didn't feel them." This is a shift. Good enough. Touch the floor again, and repeat the process. This time, ask, *what would it be like if I was 20 percent more here?*

Jeff: "I sense there's an energy circle around me; my chest and head lift up naturally. I hadn't realized I was slouching."

As you continue the process, ask, *what would it be like to be 40 percent more here?*

Jeff: "My body feels heavier, more solid. For the first time, I notice I have a back. Yet I sense more of what is in front of me than what is behind me. I still don't feel very supported. This version of me would not be good at negotiating a deal or influencing someone."

Before you begin the next level, sense/feel that just like a tree, you have roots, which extend from the bottom of your feet and spread into the ground in all directions. When you are ready ask, *what would it be like to be 60 percent more here?* When you stand, keep your attention under the earth. If it moves into your head and you find yourself thinking, try again.

Jeff: "I sense/feel the circle has expanded in equal distance 360 degrees around me. The energy radiating from my center moving forward equals the energy radiating from my back, and the space around my left and right sides feels equal. I have a new balance from which to operate. Without conscious effort, my arms reached up to the sky. It's as if they were floating or being pulled up. I feel strong and confident. Grounded."

Next, ask, *what would it be like to be 80 percent more here?*

Jeff: "I sense the roots coming from my feet have spread deeply in all directions. Upon rising, I instantly experience a greater confidence. I feel radiant. At this level, I could easily give a successful speech or resolve a conflict with a difficult client."

Last one. Ask yourself, *what would it be like if I was 100 percent here?* Remember at each level to take time to release your tensions and connect with the ground before you rise.

Jeff: "At 100 percent I feel stronger yet more flexible. I could easily handle a crisis from this version of myself. I notice my heart feels open; previously, I was unaware of my heart. I also feel connected to the world in a way I hadn't before."

The more you do this practice, the more you will sense/feel. Even if you start with a lot of mental chatter, by the time you have gone through the process, you will have made a shift. The more you practice, the easier the following shortcut that can be used at work will be.

Act "As If"

All of us do certain things that bring out the larger versions of ourselves. Felice's largest version of herself appears when she is on stage delivering a speech; she "owns the room." Joachim, a world-class musician, becomes his largest self when he lines up to the keyboard of his piano. In an instant, he's let go of his ego, attitudes, and fears and allows inspiration to move through him.

When do you experience your largest self? What's it like to be you at these times? Map out the details; for example, deep breaths in your lower belly, a strong sense of your back, feet deeply grounded, or a smile on your face. If you intimately know this larger version of yourself, you can ask for it when you need it. Then, without doubting yourself, act as if you were operating from it now.

APPLICATION FOR TEAMS

ACKNOWLEDGE THE SHADOW

When the work pressure is intense, people may operate from their smaller selves, often enabling their shadow to appear. The shadow is the unacceptable and often negative emotions and impulses of our personality like power striving, greed, envy, selfishness, and anger. The shadow is dark because it is obscured from our consciousness.

The shadow of any team member, particularly the boss, can negatively affect the team by inadvertently creating interpersonal rivalries, close-mindedness, lack of follow-through, and defensiveness. Collectively these behaviors often result in patterns of workplace behaviors, politics, procedures, structures, and organizational cultures that limit the organization and its workforce from thriving. As long as the individual and/or team are living in its shadow, creativity and breakthroughs are limited. Recognizing that we all have times when the shadow aspects of ourselves take over, the smart team accepts and prepares for those days when the boss becomes a bully or the caring creative colleague transforms into an undisciplined drama queen.

For example, in his former roles as president of San Francisco startup Cellular One, senior vice president of McCaw's Cellular One Southeast, California/Nevada regions, and then as executive VP and national build-out president of Nextel, Jim Dixon and the leadership teams he assembled made provisions for the shadow. Both in individual coaching sessions and in team meetings with consultants Chris Thorsen and Richard Moon, Dixon and his team members explored their smaller selves. Through inquiry, they identified their conditioned reactions, their anger triggers, and the subsequent behaviors that demonstrated when their shadows had taken over. Members were also asked to establish agreements or protocols regarding how they wanted to be treated when their shadows emerged. For example, did they want to be immediately confronted or did they want to take time away from each other for a day? Knowing up front how their colleagues wanted to be treated saved individuals and the team a great deal of time, energy, and aggravation. It prevented interactions that would spark and transmit the shadow from further rippling through the organization. The team also examined its collective shadow as well as that of the organization. This process helped maintain the integrity and performance of the individuals, team, and company as a whole.

SEVEN

GAIN CONTROL BY GIVING IT UP

Resolving Conflicts Harmoniously

The art of life is not controlling what happens to us, but using what happens to us.

—Gloria Steinem

On August 20, 2013, twenty-year-old Michael Brandon Hill, armed with an AK-47 and 500 rounds of ammunition, slipped through security at Ronald E. McNair Discovery Learning Academy, an elementary school in Decatur, Georgia. Once inside, he entered the front office and took bookkeeper Antoinette Tuff and others hostage. Tuff was one of three staff members who had been trained in handling hostile situations.

Hill was agitated when he walked into the office. He said he had no reason to live and that he knew this was the day he was going to die. He also said that he wanted to kill as many people as possible. Hill had a history of bipolar disease as well as a police record. He kept repeating that he was "hopeless."

He loaded his ammunition and ordered another woman to call the local television station to request a camera crew so they could film him killing police. While Tuff kept her cool, the police took up positions outside. Hill ordered her to call 911 to relay his demands that police refrain from using their radios and stop moving or he would shoot. She reported that Hill had nothing to live for and was not mentally stable. While Antoinette was on the phone, Hill fired shots into the school. No one was hurt, but Tuff knew she had to talk him down or they would all die that day.

Without confronting, blaming, or appearing afraid, she saw life from his perspective and empathetically recognized his pain. By sharing how devastated she was when her marriage of thirty-three years fell apart and that she had a son with disabilities, Antoinette forged common ground. She told him, "I went through tragedy myself. If I could recover, you can too." While Tuff worked to keep Hill calm, she signaled a code to her coworkers, who immediately alerted teachers to take the children to safety and lock their classroom doors.

Intermittently, Hill left the office and went outside to fire at police who fired back. Tuff kept talking—empathizing with his pain—and he began to open up. He told her that he hadn't taken his medication and was sick. Having shot at the police, he believed it was over for him. Antoinette assured him that was not true, since he hadn't hurt anyone, and convinced him to surrender. Before he did, he had her announce on the school intercom that he was sorry.

Antoinette's strategy of blending with Hill's perspective worked because she understood that you gain control when you give it up.

THE NATURE OF CONFLICT

Although most of us will never face this level of conflict, we all deal with it more often than we would like. According to a survey of 1,000 workers by Fierce Inc., some 30 percent of executives and employees argue with a coworker at least once a month. In one sense that is a good thing; at least it's out in the open. Can you imagine how much conflict remains hidden?

The word "conflict" is used to describe many situations. For our purpose, problems are not necessarily conflicts; neither are all disagreements conflicts. To qualify as a conflict, the participants must feel in some way threatened.

Identifying the Presenting Issue

In the midst of a financially unstable time, Jack, a senior leader of a small multimillion-dollar tech business, approached Arlene, the company president, with a question about a perceived pay inequity. The issue had to do with a major revenue stream that was in jeopardy at the time.

Arlene was under extreme pressure as she worked to save the company and everyone's job. Jack's concern for himself infuriated her. It wasn't just the question; Jack was known for his negativity and problems getting along with others. Lately, he was more vocal than usual—badmouthing some coworkers, arguing with others. Arlene had spoken with him about this a number of times, yet his behavior hadn't changed.

Thus, when she heard his latest complaint, Arlene told him in a raised voice that she was sick of his behavior. Jack responded like a scared child and said nothing. Later that day, Jack, who feared for his job, approached her to try to work things out. Instead of discussing the issue, Arlene told him everything was okay. Things went downhill from there.

For two weeks they barely spoke except when absolutely essential. When Jack tried to maintain the contact, Arlene didn't engage; in fact, she started questioning him about his projects in a way that made him very uncomfortable. According to Arlene, she discovered that Jack was spending a great deal of time on unnecessary projects. Finally, a shell-shocked Jack was fired and escorted out of the building.

In most conflicts, the difference between points of view may not be the same as the perceived difference. Often, the participants significantly misunderstand the core issue. Antonio Piazza, an internationally recognized master of mediation, confirms this: "Even in cases involving immense sums that have been litigated for years . . . , the opening session of the mediation is often the first time that the decision makers clearly hear the main points of the other side's position."

Identifying the Deeper Issue

Beneath the presenting problem, there often is a deeper issue—the individual's emotional need for safety and acceptance that is filtered by personality type, culture, gender, and experience. Consequently, even if you solve the presenting problem, without directly or indirectly resolving the deeper issue, it will recur in different ways.

To identify and understand the deeper issue, you must go beyond classifying people as good or bad, even if their behavior infuriates you. That path leads to fighting. Instead, if you think of the person as a work-in-progress and look deeper, you will find qualities and skills that might benefit you and the team; at the very least, it makes the conflict easier to resolve.

Although the presenting problem was the pay inequity, Jack sensed he was not part of Arlene's inner circle. In his view, he was told he was being negative and disruptive whenever his perspective differed from that of the COO, Arlene's closest ally.

Jack is a Type 5 personality: intellectually smart but not very emotionally savvy or sensitive to others' feelings. Thus, how he delivers his message and his frequent negativity lead to misunderstanding. He deeply wants to be included and accepted unconditionally. Jack recognizes these challenges and says he wants to grow and change; however, he needs the help and support of Arlene and the team.

Arlene, for her part, had only been president for two years, during which time she had not only been dealing with internal and external challenges, she had inherited a dysfunctional team that frustrated her. Team accountability was inconsistent, communication and follow-up were often lacking, and the team was divided into "us and them" fac-

A Seed of Truth

*"In a controversy, the instant we feel anger,
we have already ceased striving for truth and
have begun striving for ourselves."*

—ABRAHAM J. HESCHEL

tions. Members badmouthed one another and, at times, were downright disrespectful to one another. Unable to resolve these issues, Arlene, a Type 2 who was accustomed to forging strong relationships and teams, was overwhelmed and unsure of whom to trust. Instead of maintaining her own positive attitude, she became mired in the organization's negativity. As a result, she was sometimes unable to detach in order to make wise team decisions. Arlene, the helper, needed help from her team and wasn't getting it. Feeling out of control and angry, she focused on Jack, whom she identified as the main problem. Get rid of him, she figured, and a large part of her problem was solved. Clearly, neither Jack nor Arlene understood the other's perspective.

REACTIONS TO CONFLICT

When we view conflict as negative, we resist it by attacking as Arlene did, collapse under its pressure, or freeze as Jack did. If we perceive it as a contest, we attach our egos and self-worth to whether or not we win. Those who collapse or freeze forfeit their voice; therefore, their point of view, which might help resolve the conflict, is never heard. Those who resist the pressure by fighting for their point of view fail to see that even if they win, they lose.

Over time whoever loses may stew in righteous indignation and seek ways to get even or, conversely, may choose to let bygones be bygones, but the person's regard for "the winner" plummets. When Richard Parsons was transitioning from chairman of Citigroup to CEO and principal dealmaker of Time Warner, Steve Ross, who once ran Time Warner, told him:

> "Remember that this is a small business and a long life. You are going to see all these guys come around and around again, so how you treat them on each individual transaction is going to make an impression in the long haul. When you do deals, leave a little something to make everyone happy instead of trying to grab every nickel off the table."

Sharing what he learned from Ross, Parsons said:

> "I've used that advice a thousand times literally. Most people in business do not follow that though . . . I think people get hung up with their advisers, investment bankers, lawyers, and others, and every instance becomes a tug of war to see who can outduel the other to get the slightest little advantage on a transaction. But people don't keep in mind that the advisers are going to move on to the next deal, while you and I are going to have to see each other again.[1]

If, however, we perceive conflict neither negatively nor positively, but as Thomas Crum, author of *The Magic of Conflict,* does, as the "interference of a pattern of energies,"[2] we can view it as a learning experience. Conflict then becomes, as Crum states, "nature's prime motivator for change."[3] To do this, you have to be willing to give up control.

Giving Up Control

This does not mean allowing yourself to be victimized or resigning yourself to the situation or giving up your competitive edge, values, or passion. Similarly, gaining control is not the same as being aggressive or

Table 7-1. How each Enneagram type responds to pressure.

	BEHAVIOR UNDER PRESSURE	BEHAVIOR IN OVERWHELMING STRESS
Type 1 The Perfectionist	• Free time causes anxiety; pleasure is eliminated from the schedule. • Work becomes compulsive; they do what they SHOULD do rather than what they WANT to do. • Inner critic becomes increasingly punitive. Right or wrong thinking intensifies. • Making decisions and completing important tasks is difficult. • Emotional control tightens; resentment grows.	• Move from super control of inner rage to profoundly emotional. Envy, melancholy, anger erupt. • Feel victimized by people who don't understand the importance of order and values. • Move from optimism about enhancing the greater good to despair about effecting change. • Move from detailed criticism of others to self-absorbed hopelessness about prospects.
Type 2 The Helper	• Overextending themselves results in helpfulness that is intrusive or controlling. • Worry about what others think. Work harder and more relentlessly for recognition. • Become impatient from increasingly superficial emotional connections. • Have short bursts of irritability and/or crying.	• Feel victimized by other people's abuse, insensitivity, stupidity, or the lack of empathy and appreciation. • Become forceful, aggressive, and/or argumentative. • Dismiss others' feelings and points of view. • Directly confront, threaten, and/or punish people for ingratitude, lack of response, or perceived wrongs. • Move to control and dominate. • Act out feelings of rage and betrayal.

Type 3 The Performer	• Attention narrows to the tasks at hand, which blunt feelings of anxiety. • Practice extreme workaholism. • Become inefficiently efficient; cut corners in places that matter. • Create stress and conflict in relationships; become impatient. • Soften the truth with partial truths; become an instant expert. • Are intolerant of criticism.	• Feel victimized by events they can't control. • Move from focused intent to loss of concentration; from big projects to small tasks, errands, details, and inessentials; from fast action to paralysis that results from trying to include everyone's views. • Persevere, but disengage. • May become disillusioned with life and themselves during major setbacks.
Type 4 The Romantic	• Withdraw and become the outsider. • Become increasingly competitive. "Seduce and reject" style intensifies. Find fault with others. • Mood swings increase/ efficiency decreases/ feelings of grief and abandonment deepen/ fall into inaction/ become self-absorbed, temperamental, and sarcastic/may create emotional scenes.	• Move towards others as a way to compensate for the problems their behavior has created. • Slightly forced friendliness emerges; try too hard to fix things. • Conceal needs by focusing on the needs of others. Feel they've sold themselves out by focusing on others. • Exaggerate their importance in people's lives/seek credit for accomplishments while complaining how unappreciated they are.

Type 5 The Observer	• Shrink inward: withhold emotions, energy, and data/isolate/daydream. • Become tense, intellectually arrogant, and disapproving. • Have secretive/compartmentalized life. • May become uncooperative/"beyond" the need to explain themselves.	• Become terrified by having to wing it and deal with multiple choices. • Feel more alienated as people. Don't see past their sociable façade. • Thinking speeds up; confusion increases. • Have fear of being sucked into people's agendas. • Attention scatters in a frantic effort to find solutions/display ungrounded enthusiasm and talk nonstop.
Type 6 The Trooper	• Feel dread/worst case scenarios dominate thinking. Disbelieve their capacities and decisions. • Practice contrary thinking. • Complain and blame others without taking any definitive action. • Feel victimized/want to be rescued.	• If the energy goes into tasks, it is constructive; if into worst case scenarios, it's terrifying. • Become driven and potentially workaholic/tense. • Make additional efforts to fit in/ become more image conscious. • Become boastful, self-promoting. • Become dismissive of others/adopt condescending attitudes, and/or hype their own superiority.

Type 7 The Epicure	• Reframe situations positively in an effort to avoid feeling fear. • Become impulsive. • Procrastinate due to multiple options. • Make exaggerated promissory plans that terminate in poor follow-through. • Are extremely demanding and impatient with self and others the more anxious they become. • Have more problems with details. • May not equally share the workload.	• Begin to restrain themselves, work harder, believe only they can do the job. • Move from easygoing to autocratic; from multiple options to one right way to do things. • Attempt to educate others. • Have tendency to debate or critique others' views. • Become short, impersonal, and highly impatient with any degree of incompetence. • Become angry, sarcastic, and resentful/scold and/or nitpick.
Type 8 The Boss	• Increase self-assertive/confrontational style/fight to win/blame others. • "My way or the highway"/dismiss other points of view. • Deny weakness, fear, doubt, or indecision/don't want to back down. • Test to see how others handle pressure. • Are intolerant of ambiguity and deceit.	• Fear that power source has dried up. • Detach and become quiet/reflect, read/become more informed in order to size up situation and make decisions. • Become deeply preoccupied and secretive about their plans. • May become high-strung over time.

| Type 9 The Mediator | • Downplay their choices and desires/appease people/seek peace at any price.
• Retreat inside themselves/daydream/ become absentminded/ emotionally numb.
• Do the less essential things rather than the important ones.
• Procrastinate/postpone being fully present.
• Express anger in indirect, passive ways.
• Become more stubborn. | • Feel themselves the victim of small-minded, argumentative people with secret agendas.
• Move from worry, panic, and paralysis to intense focus on work and frantic activity.
• Have doubts and long-held complaints against others; blame others.
• Have angry outbursts/ fight for their own interests. |

resistant. True control comes from remaining centered, connected, and open to learning while, at the same time, accepting reality. It is recognizing that perhaps you are not seeing the whole picture and that by insisting on your point of view, you limit your engagement and yourself. As organizational consultant Andrew Cohn points out, the statement "Isn't this interesting" is one of the most masterful statements you can make. It frees your attention, which may be passionately tied to some position, and sharpens your perception. As Andrew suggests, it shifts you into a learning mindset that is essential for resolving conflicts harmoniously.

Most of us struggle with the issue of control. We may say that we are not concerned with control yet our behavior, particularly under pressure, often defies our words. In fact, the feeling that we are losing control can be extremely stressful. To stay safe and secure, each of us seeks to control our environment to differing degrees. Yet, each personality type approaches gaining control differently (see Table 7-1 on previous pages). In usual day-to-day situations, Type 1s do what is right, 2s help others, 3s perform, 4s compare themselves to others, 5s get more information, 6s look to authority, 7s entertain, 8s speak loudly and act aggressively, and 9s get out of the way. As the pressure builds, behavior patterns change. It's important to remember that not everyone with a given personality type reacts identically. Behavior also has a lot to do with self-awareness and personal development. Those who are very evolved may rarely revert to the predicted behaviors while those who are least developed may be more extreme.

Ultimately, no matter our tactics, we discover that "control" is fleeting and more an illusion than a fact. Although we may require people to do as we dictate, rarely do we control them. Consider the question James Jordan, currently the Pennsylvania executive director of the National Alliance on Mental Illness, poses: "What is the most beautiful thing you can think of? The thing that means life itself. The thing without which, life cannot exist."

The answer is breath.

Without air, there is no life. However, if you tried to control and hold onto it because it is so valuable, you would die. You have to let it go and breathe in and out. You have to share your breath and allow it to blend and become one with the atmosphere. I try to live by that concept. Whenever possible I move away from judging others and trying to control situations so that I can blend with and thus understand the other person's perspective.

Understanding the Other Person's Point of View

Not long ago, in response to a conversation we had about conflict, a friend sent me an email that said, "Someone I respect once told me there are only two things a person could do during a conflict . . . fight or flee, and the choice depended on who or what has to be protected." In the school hostage situation described earlier, Antoinette Tuff saw another option. She went with the energy of the situation and by blending with the perspective of the troubled young man, Michael Brandon Hill, was able to lead him in a new direction, thus saving her life and those of others.

When we create a blend, our attention is located inside ourselves but expands to include the other person. In that way, we are able to pick up their energetic intentions and to understand their emotions and point of view more clearly. Blending is not the same as merging. In merging you lose your self-reference while in blending you maintain it. As Richard Moon, aikidoist and founder of extraordinarylistening.com, pointed out to me, "Blend with them and you then have the jurisdiction to lead. But if you are truly blending it's not really about you leading them or them leading you. Instead, you go into synergy and the whole leads both of you."

When we blend, we accept our situation rather than fight or flee. That doesn't mean that we agree with or like what's happening. In fact, we may see a better way and want to make a change. However, resolving conflict is not about who is right but about acknowledging our differences and learning to use them in service of the greater good. As author and martial artist Thomas Crum points out, "A willingness to accept another's truth does not invalidate our own."[4]

Consider the previously discussed conflict between Arlene, a company president, and Jack, a senior leader. If Arlene chose to blend with Jack, she would first accept that he has an idea, a flow of energy, he thinks is important. Instead of taking his comments personally, being wounded by them, and responding defensively, she would listen carefully and would figuratively turn to see the world from Jack's perspective. By asking questions such as "why is this important to you?" she would understand his point of view so well that she could state his case and see the seeds of truth in it, no matter how large or small they were.

If Arlene were truly present, she would sense the moment when she could lead Jack in a new direction so that he might see her point of view. In going back and forth, they would be sharing the gifts of their perspectives. The more they understood each other's point of view, the more likely they would be to find common and higher ground, which offers a solution that is better than either could imagine. This is aikido's win-win approach to conflict resolution.

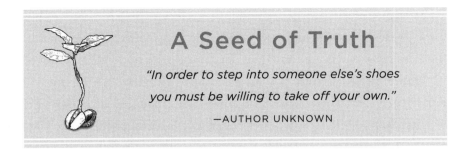

A Seed of Truth

*"In order to step into someone else's shoes
you must be willing to take off your own."*

—AUTHOR UNKNOWN

THE AIKI MODEL OF CONFLICT RESOLUTION

The principles of aikido translate brilliantly to resolving verbal conflicts (Figure 7-1).

What follows is a seven-step model.

Step 1: The Conflict Occurs

Sometimes all it takes is a word, a look, or a deed to spark irritation. At other times, a history of disappointments or frustrations where you ei-

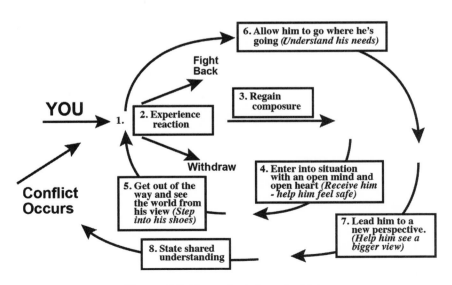

Figure 7-1. The principles of aikido.

ther said nothing or saw no change in the other person's behavior triggers the concern. Then there are times when competition for scarce resources or different expectations or standards kicks off the conflict.

No matter what triggers us, at the first sign of conflict, a rush of energy comes into our system and sets off a biological reaction. The thalamus sends part of the stimulus to the neocortex, the thinking brain, as well as to the amygdala, which plays a key role in the processing of emotions. According to Daniel Goleman, author of *Emotional Intelligence,* the amygdala is sometimes "hijacked." A fight, flight, or freeze situation triggers the hypothalmic–pituitary–adrenal (HPA) axis and overpowers the rational mind—the amygdala—which causes us to respond immediately and more intensely than the actual stimulus requires. "In the midst of a disagreement between a leader and his subordinate," Andrew Cohn of Lighthouse Consulting told me, "the leader became so angry that his lip began to quiver and he couldn't think straight." That's the effect of a hijacked amygdala.

Step 2: Experience the Reaction

Assuming your amygdala has not been hijacked when the first verbal arrow pierces you, sensations and emotions arise. Your thinking mind interprets these feelings, often weaving stories of injustice, anger, and/or pain based on your past experience. Yet to resolve the conflict you need an empty mind in order to perceive clearly and deeply. Therefore, when the conflict begins, step into the resolution process with the detachment of a researcher. Pause and notice without making a judgment of what is going in your mind/body/energy field. Ask yourself:

- Where do I feel the tightness or pressure in my system?
- Can I feel my back and my feet on the ground?
- How much space do I occupy?
- What emotion do I feel?
- What thoughts are associated with these feelings and sensations?

Step 3: Regain Composure

Once you recognize that you've left that place within you I call "home," it's time to return to yourself by unraveling and gathering all the streams of attention that have become entwined in the conflict. It means breathing deeply in a rhythm that your body innately knows. Regaining your composure is about letting go of the attachment to your story, thoughts, and biases as well as to the particular way your body tenses. It means giving up resistance in order to find your center/ground, which is always there to welcome and support you.

Step 4: Enter

When attacking, Aikido students learn: How you go in is how you go out. If you attack hard, the fall you take when you are thrown is hard. If you come in fast, you leave fast. The same is true of verbal conflicts. If you enter the conflict enraged, you'll probably leave that way. If you go into the conflict seeing the other person as your enemy, you'll probably leave the situation with that person feeling the same way about you. Thus, who you are—the version of you that enters the conflict—is enormously important as it sets the stage for what will occur. Do you enter as a person of peace or as a vengeful warrior?

Release Your Inner Fighter

At a presentation to members of the graduate engineering department at UC Berkeley, Tony Piazza, a lawyer specializing in mediation and the man *Business Week* says has "a knack for bringing parties together in deals where the situation seems intractable,"[5] delivered a presentation he calls "The Physics of Fighting." He begins by introducing a paradox, and, as he speaks, he bounces a handball.

Tony explains that by the time they come to him, the people whose disputes he mediates—smart, highly successful businesspeople—have usually invested time, energy, and many millions without resolving the dispute. Indeed, often they are further apart than when they began. Still, he says, eight out of ten leave his office after one day with an agreement. "Why," he asked his audience, "are they getting such a dramatically different result . . . ?"

While still bouncing the ball, he tells this group of engineers that the answer comes from the physics of what they are viewing at that moment—gravity. We tend to think of gravity as the force attracting objects towards the center of the planet, yet every particle of matter in the universe attracts every other particle of matter in the universe to it. What makes the ball bounce up is explained by Newton's third law: *For every action there is always an equal and opposite reaction.* The paradox, he explained, is that every particle of matter yearns to reconnect with every other particle of matter and, at the same time, every particle of matter is reacting and driving every other particle away. Thus, although the reality is that everything is connected, we retain the "the illusion of separation." We experience both fear and desire: We want this; we're afraid of that. Piazza believes this is not an accident. He says, "We designed it this way, precisely so that we get to face all of our fears and desires, and find the courage to see past the illusion of separation and open up to the underlying unity."

Mediation works because it provides a less reactive environment in which the parties are no longer at the mercy of Newton's law, one in which they can evaluate and discuss options. Therefore, they are no longer reacting to/fighting with one another and can find agreement.

You may not have Tony's expertise; however, you can enter conflict with the intention of letting go of the fighter within so you can become more peaceful. You can also engage in techniques for resolving conflict that, if performed with awareness, will help you identify what triggers your inner fighter so you may learn to prevent it. Here's how to begin:

- Move towards the conflict with an attitude of openhearted interest. Trust yourself enough to be vulnerable. Assume a positive attitude; don't be defensive, fearful, angry, or avoidant.

- Share with the other person how you feel about addressing this issue. Are you nervous or fearful going into this process?
- Take turns stating the problem and paraphrasing what you heard. Remember, your versions of the problem may vary wildly. Just listening nonjudgmentally to how the other person views the problem may reveal common ground and ways to resolve the conflict. Don't look for solutions yet. Concentrate on sharing your needs and let the process unwind.
- State your intentions and expectations about the outcome of the dialogue. They, too, may differ. That's okay. Let go of control; allow the process to lead you.
- Determine if you have a shared interest in maintaining the relationship; without it, resolving the conflict may be very difficult.

Step 5: Create a Space for Confluence

According to Webster's dictionary, "confluence" is the flowing together of two or more streams. Yet in most conflict, there is little confluence between the participants' streams of energies, thoughts, and perspectives. Typically, both parties enter the conflict with preconceived ideas, emotional baggage, and the staunch belief that they are right. Instead of listening carefully, they frame what they want to say while the other person speaks. Interruptions and tones of voice repel rather than welcome.

The aiki model of conflict resolution seeks to change this by first establishing a safe environment. This begins with respecting the other person. Respect is transmitted not only through the words you use and through your voice tone, but also through your body language and presence. In the example described earlier, Jack never felt safe discussing his concerns directly with Arlene. At the first sign of disapproval, he would back off. Because he couldn't freely discuss the issues, he leaked them to his coworkers, which created a negative environment.

Creating a safe environment includes understanding and acknowledging the other person's interests, needs, and feelings, whether or not you agree with them. It helps to ask yourself to whom the other person needs to look good and what you can do to make that happen.

Last, but definitely not least, listen with care. Take ten seconds before you respond. If the person's statement sets off emotional triggers, take time to compose yourself and come back to neutral. Paraphrase to help make the person feel understood and ask that person to do the same for you. Listen not just with your ears but with your whole body. Listen not only to the other person, but also to your own intuition. Let the way you listen reflect an unprotected openness, free of fear and restrictions. Listen with kindness and compassion. You'd be amazed at its power to heal the separation that exists within all conflicts.

Step 6: Don't Assume You Know Where the Person Is Going

Once you've created a safe environment, you're ready to deeply inquire into the other person's point of view. This is the heart of the blend, and it offers the possibility of true connection and learning. To reap these gifts requires that you constantly shed your biases, beliefs, and egocentric thoughts in order to listen clearly. Instead of thinking you know what the other person is going to say or what the person means, pose your assumptions as questions rather than dogmatic statements and explain the reasoning behind your assumptions. Sounds simple, but it's not.

Arlene, for example, told Jack many times that he needed to get along well with others, yet he never truly understood what she meant. He never asked because he believed that he needed her permission to question her. He believed it was intrusive and feared he would be attacked for it. Arlene added to the conflict because she assumed he understood her and never clarified the change she required.

Sometimes people resist or don't ask questions because they don't know the "right" questions to ask. The good news is that you don't need brilliant questions to resolve a conflict. All you need are some probers—"Why is that important to you?" . . . "Help me understand" . . . "Tell me

A Seed of Truth

"The more you know about another person's story, the less possible it is to see that person as your enemy."

—PARKER PALMER

more"—to encourage the other people to move deeper into their concerns and needs. Probers help to peel the onion in order to uncover the core issue.

In a proficient blend, you've heard the other person's point of view and have paraphrased it to show acknowledgment. Once you've stepped into the other person's shoes and walked the same path, an opportunity will arise when you can easily turn the other person around and show him your perspective.

Step 7: Leading the Other Person

Now it's time for you to state your own perspective. Too often, though, the conversation begins with *Yes, I've heard you BUT* . . . where BUT is a dismissal of the other person's ideas that creates resistance. To lead someone to a different point of view, use AND: *I hear you AND here's how I see it.*

When advocating your point of view, make your reasoning explicit. Explain how you came to your perspective and include the data you used. Invite the other person to explore your perspective. If you don't hold your opinion sacred, you will leave space for the other person to offer gaps in your thinking. This is an important part of the process because it may elevate your thinking. Win-win solutions will be revealed if you are both open-minded and willing to see the fuller picture by going back and forth in this manner. By giving up control, you will gain a new sense of security and discover the joy of collaboration and communion.

ADVICE

Someone dancing inside us
has learned only a few steps:
The "Do-Your-Work" in 4/4 time,
the "What-Do-You-Expect" waltz.
He hasn't noticed yet the woman
standing away from the lamp,
the one with black eyes
who knows the rumba
and strange steps in jumpy rhythms
from the mountains of Bulgaria.
If they dance together,
something unexpected will happen;
If they don't, the next world
will be a lot like this one.

—Bill Holm[6]

Learn True Collaboration

Most of the time what we call collaboration in the workplace is really the coordination of resources. Most collaborative team gatherings are just another meeting. Rarely do we walk away energized by or with new ideas.

True collaboration is a process that creates new possibilities and opportunities that wouldn't otherwise exist by creating an identify shift in the participants and the group. An elevated identity arises when the energy of fighting dissipates and a true interest in learning emerges. Inquiry opens the space for insights and unlikely connections to be revealed. This upgrade requires the lessening of ego habits that preserve the status quo and keeps the conversation familiar and manageable. The ego wants to feel safe, thus it avoids or resists difficult feedback. When we act from ego, we blame external circumstances or others instead of taking responsibility. We focus on short term rather than long term and serve our smaller self rather than the greater good.

However, when pressure is used to elevate rather than to compete or fight, that energy upgrades us, thereby enabling us to hold the space so new ideas and qualities can emerge. Communion, which is the act of sharing or holding common thoughts, emotions, and/or energies, can then occur. When Tony Piazza mediates, he not only expertly identifies and verbally helps people work though their concerns, he also nonverbally holds the space of peace so that the bounce from desire for connection to its opposite reaction does not take place. His presence invites participants, who may not consciously recognize the deeper energy state, to join him in this centered, peaceful state. In most cases they are positively affected by it and many are able to open to it and operate from it.

Stress, at home or at work, dissipates when true communion occurs. Although we may pride ourselves for being self-made people, sensing our connections and knowing that there are those in our lives who provide a safe place for us are priceless. The ability to turn pressure from an enemy into an ally grows when we realize that nobody does it alone.

PERSONAL PRACTICE

FINDING THE CORE ISSUE WITHIN THE CONFLICT

Conflicts are not only about differences in perspectives; on a deeper level they are about our limited personal belief systems, which become obvious when we are under pressure. You may believe, for example, that you are safe when you are in control or if you are performing perfectly or winning. When these beliefs are jeopardized, emotions run high and you lose your center/ground. Your attention then splits between resolving the issue and defending yourself by blaming, belittling, and/or telling stories about how the other person wronged you. Although you may be right to question the other person's intent, thinking, or actions, getting stuck in a mental loop of blame drains your energy and keeps you a victim. However, bringing your attention back inside yourself in order to identify and modify your limited belief empowers you. Conflict then becomes a gift that helps you understand another person and yourself.

I call the process of identifying the limited belief "peeling the onion to find the pain." Every conflict has so many levels of truth that to find what triggers our emotional upheaval requires that we peel away the layers to get to the core issue. To do this, first, name the presenting problem. Then ask yourself such questions as what else is going on, what's underneath that level of truth, why is it important to you. Approach this process without judgment, blame, or shame. When you think you've reached the core issue that is generating your pain, notice if your emotional reaction to the conflict has dissipated. If so, you've identified it. If not, keep peeling the onion. When you identify the core of your pain, it frees your energy and empowers you to address the conflict with more power, understanding, and compassion.

For example, Angela, an operations director, was furious with her boss because she believed her bonus was too small. When I spoke to her about this, she hadn't talked with her boss about her bonus because she was too upset. Only when Angela realized the extent to which this conflict was negatively affecting the way she felt about her work was she willing to examine its cause. When she peeled the onion, she discovered layers of pain that resulted from:

- Not getting fair share when bonuses were disbursed
- Not being included in decisions about bonus disbursement
- Not being treated as an equal by men on team
- Being the only team member in specific instances not publicly recognized for her contributions to the organization
- Thinking things would not change

In addition, she was:

- Afraid to rock the boat
- Afraid of ruining her relationships with the other team members and her boss
- Afraid they wouldn't like her . . . BINGO!!!

Once Angela named the issue beneath the presenting problem, it lost some of its power. We were able to calmly discuss how to approach and talk to her boss about the inequities she experienced. Her boss apologized for some of the inequities and promised to make some changes. He also explained that he gave her a lower bonus because, from his perspective, Angela's defensive attitude limited her teammates' willingness to collaborate with her. Therefore, she had been less successful than they were.

Angela recognized that there was some truth in that and worked on shifting her behavior. A year later, I checked in with her and her boss, and discovered she no longer let her fear of being disliked control her and was no longer defensive. She had reached out to her teammates, which led to better collaboration. The following year, Angela told me her bonus was very fair. By looking inside herself, she created a win–win for everyone.

APPLICATION FOR TEAMS

REDUCE CONFLICT AND ENHANCE COLLABORATION
BY CHANGING THE WORKPLACE ENVIRONMENT

Like so many companies, at Citrix Fort Lauderdale senior managers fought over resources. They bickered over the number of people on their teams, who was entitled to the corner offices, and even who got what furniture. Collaboration was a chronic problem, and silos needed to be broken down. As in most traditional organizations, people only knew their teammates and those in nearby offices or cubicles. Often their offices or cubicles weren't even near those with whom they needed to collaborate.

The technology industry tends to attract a personality type that views information as power and thus doesn't always want to share it. They are not interested in small talk and prefer not to interact with others unless it is vital to their interest. Therefore, something radical was required to reduce conflict among senior managers and enhance collaboration throughout the division.

Michael McKiernan, vice president of business technology, who was hired to fix the problem, did exactly that. He realized that on any given day only 54 percent of the expensive office space was used. So, he tore down the office walls, removed the cubicles, and created an open floor plan, which allowed the 350 employees to utilize all of the space. He created town squares equipped with coffee and snack bars where people could work. The shared space encourages those who are often reclusive to interact more with others. People have an opportunity to converse, learn about each other's projects, and share ideas and knowledge. Teams may choose to hold their meetings in the town square. By sharing space with associates from other departments, they got to know each other, and the silos have significantly dissolved.

Those who want a more quiet space may work in the space called the "library" or use a private room. However, the rule is that they may not use the private room day after day and, therefore, must at times be in a position to interact and collaborate.

The new "work anywhere" format has eliminated some of the workplace stress. They are no longer watched by supervisors to see if they are being productive, which eliminated busy work. They are evaluated by results, not by the amount of time they spend at work. Nor do they need to be concerned if someone sees them using the Internet for a personal reason. Michael, recognizing that work and personal life are not mutually exclusive, has created a space that supports both.

As the "work anywhere" model is still relatively new at Citrix Fort Lauderdale, some who are accustomed to having their own space are still acclimating to it, but most have embraced it. Half of the people who were telecommuting stopped because the new environment is more fun. According to a Citrix survey, 46 percent of their employees say they are more productive, happier, and more collaborative.

EIGHT

NOBODY DOES IT ALONE

Taking Your Heart to Work

*When we seek for connection, we restore the world to whole-
ness. Our seemingly separate lives become meaningful as we
discover how truly necessary we are to each other.*

—Margaret Wheatley

n her autobiography, *Living History,* Hillary Rodham Clinton re-
called how devastated she felt when the Democrats lost both houses
of Congress in the 1994 midterm elections. Mrs. Clinton blamed
herself for the failure of health care reform, and realized that she had
become a lightning rod for some people's anger. She considered with-
drawing from actively participating in political and policy work.

When she told women colleagues about her disappointment and
guilt, they reminded her of her value to the administration and that she
was a role model for a generation of young women. Their encourage-
ment and support helped Hillary regain her confidence and, as you
know, she went on to become a senator and then secretary of state.[1]
Whether you are an elite power broker or an ordinary Joe, to varying
degrees, we need each other. The story of the self-made person is just

that—a story. When you delve deeper, you find there was help along the way. Nobody does it alone.

In the roughest times, the emotional support of those who care provides us with a soft place to land. Their kindness says we matter and helps us see our authentic selves. It alleviates our stress and self-doubt. It energizes us. We all need to be seen, heard, and supported. Nowhere do we need this more than in the workplace, where competition rather than cooperation is often the norm. In this chapter my focus is on what it means to bring your heart to work and what you can do to create a safe environment in which you can thrive and contribute your best. We will also look at organizations that have created cultures that support caring and kindness. We'll begin by examining how emotions create well-being or stress and why creating a caring workplace is smart business.

EMOTIONS AND YOUR PHYSICAL AND MENTAL HEALTH

Though we may complain about high levels of stress at work, rarely do we discuss our emotions in the workplace. Afraid of being vulnerable, looking weak, being misunderstood, or seen as unprofessional, many of us adopt a "don't let them see me sweat" attitude. Much of our stress comes from the accumulation of emotions—fear, anger, hurt, and others—that we fail to acknowledge to ourselves, let alone try to resolve with our boss or colleagues. This can have serious effects on our health.

After analyzing one hundred studies, Howard Friedman, professor at the University of California Riverside, reported that being chronically depressed, anxious, pessimistic, irritated, or critical actually doubles a person's chances of developing a major disease. These negative emotions change our blood chemistry, which in turn clogs our arteries, raises our blood pressure and cholesterol levels, and weakens our immune system. However, people who are emotionally positive are much less susceptible to becoming ill. As Dr. Joel Levey and Michelle Levey say in *Living in Balance,* "Their hearts and brains exhibit far more balanced, coherent, and energy efficient functioning. . . . The key to this lies not in the words people say or the affirmations they tell themselves but in the genuineness and authenticity of their attitudes and feelings."[2] Caring, research shows, is good for our physical and mental health.

Matthieu Ricard, a French Buddhist monk and right-hand man to the Dalai Lama, participated in a clinical study at the University of Wisconsin that measured happiness by comparing the relative activation of the left prefrontal cortex with the right prefrontal cortex. Ricard's measurements were well outside the normal parameter, making him the happiest person they'd measured. When asked what he was thinking while being measured, he said he was meditating on compassion. According to Matthieu, his brain scans mirror his personal experience that compassion is the happiest state.

IT'S GOOD BUSINESS: CARING IN THE WORKPLACE

It turns out that caring and positive emotions are good for business. A 1999 Gallup research study[3] found that having a best friend at work was one of the twelve traits of highly productive workgroups. Employees who reported having a best friend at work are more loyal to their companies and have a higher retention rate. Among other data, the research also showed that those with a best friend at work were more likely to have been praised at work, that they have more support for their professional development, and that they believe their opinion when expressed at work matters.

Furthermore, the study showed that, even though they experience the same amount of stress as their coworkers, employees who have best friends at work have a much higher ability to manage the stress.

In addition, when employees are in a positive mood they are more likely to help coworkers and provide better customer service. Positive emotions are also associated with increases in positive supervisory evaluations, higher income, enhanced negotiating ability, and more employees voluntarily performing discretionary acts for the benefit of the organization. Caring, compassion, and other positive emotions imply higher productivity and lower insurance, workers' compensation, and turnover costs.[4]

Little wonder then that smart companies are attempting to weave care, connection, and fun into the fabric of their organization's culture in order to enhance engagement while decreasing stress. Furthermore, customers like to buy from those who not only give them a good deal, but whose personnel convey a positive attitude; caring can also equate to increased sales.

Companies have many different strategies to encourage employees to bring their hearts to work. Some honor care as a corporate value. Others install caring structures—gyms, tennis courts, credit unions, employee assistance programs, yoga, and meditation classes—as a sign of their concern for people. Some offer free food, have "bring your pet to work" days, and demonstrate family friendliness by offering day care and flex time. Still others train their managers in emotional intelligence, advocate inclusive decision making, and reward high performance monetarily and with time off.

Despite these workplace improvements, companies in the United States lose $350 billion annually in lost production.[5] That's because most of the improvements are external mechanisms. Although employees like the free food, tennis courts, and yoga classes, many view them as a way organizations control employees and keep them on campus so they will work more. Many employees doubt that their organizations care about them and have a cautious and sometimes rigid view of bringing their hearts to work. Given corporate politics, some consider it dangerous to let down their guard and authentically connect with care. One executive told me, "We're viewed on dollars; though our mission talks about caring for people, our bonuses are connected to our results. No one considers how we treat people when they are dividing up the money." Here is what another manager confided:

"People will step on you to get what they want. The same bosses who are so pleasant and considerate with their higher-ups can do a complete 180 when it comes to dealing with their employees. My current boss can be rigid, aggressive, and insensitive at times. Though I've learned to have a thick skin, he doesn't consider how his behavior affects the quality of work life, people's stress levels, and their self-esteem."

As these comments illustrate, a gap often exists between the organization's perception of how well they care for their workforce and the employees' perceptions. Yet, some companies get it right. They teach associates on all levels how to enhance their emotional intelligence, how to be smarter about feelings. They help employees link their work to the broader work and values of the organization. In so doing, employees perceive meaning in their work and feel that they are making a difference. Through connection and care, they build trust, compassion, and the desire to serve the greater good.

More Than Lip Service: An Organization That Got It Right

In the mid-1990s before First Union National Bank was bought by Wachovia, A.G. (Buddy) Johnson, the area president in Broward County, Florida, decided to create an organizational culture based on caring, authenticity, oneness, communication, trust, and empowerment. While so many executives at that time didn't understand the value of caring, Buddy understood that caring increased engagement and productivity, which in turn positively affected the bottom line. As part of his culture change initiative, he decided that at Christmas the bank was going to provide for the special needs of its workforce. To avoid embarrassment, employees could make a request without having to explain their need. The bank's Family Council—composed of people at different levels throughout the organization—was responsible for reviewing and responding to the requests. All went well until the council received a request for a VCR, which many considered inappropriate. Where were the boundaries? Was the bank being exploited?

After much thought, they decided to grant the request. If they were wrong and the bank was being exploited, the financial damage was minimal; if they denied the request, the message of mistrust they would be sending would ripple throughout the organization, undermine the bank's core values, and cause damage not easily repaired. It was later discovered that the request came from a woman with a sick child who was unable to attend school and received video instruction.

A Paradigm Shift: What a Caring Company Can Be

Many of us would like to work in organizations with heart. We want to feel emotionally safe. We want to trust that our vulnerability will not be exploited and that others are there for us if we need them. When a workplace is infused with heart, it unites people and creates a sense of belonging. From this authentic union of heart, a shared story that speaks to the greater good and the goodness of each individual is born. Who we are and the gifts and talents we contribute are appreciated, and we are moved to perform our work with joy, passion, and even laughter. In these organizations, pressure helps us thrive rather than depletes us. As wellsprings of care, they inspire and nurture us to be our larger selves and to produce our best work.

Try to think past your experience and conventional wisdom, and imagine what such a workplace would look and feel like. It would not be you *against* the others; instead you would see yourself *in* the others. You would recognize both their imperfections and their greatness, you would treat them with the kindness and respect you want for yourself; you would support their successes; and you would extend compassion and empathy when they faced challenges. And they would do the same for you because each person recognizes that you are in it together.

You might think that's never going to happen. There is too much corporate politics; too many people are power hungry, arrogant, and egocentric; too many people want to squash you in order to get ahead;

and too many people say nothing because they don't want to get involved. Well, you might be right. Then again, you might not. Attitudes seem to be shifting, and compassion as a living virtue is showing up where you least expect it.

A CARING VISION IN ACTION

When Greg Fischer was inaugurated as mayor of Louisville, Kentucky, a city of approximately 750,000 people, he declared three objectives. The first was for the city to become healthier—physically, emotionally, socially, and spiritually; the second was for the city to embrace lifelong learning; and the third was for Louisville to be a caring, compassionate city. On November 11, 2011, he signed a resolution committing Louisville to a ten-year Compassionate City Campaign, which meant that Louisville was recognized along with Seattle and Houston as an International Compassionate City[6] and a member of the Compassionate Action Network.[7] To help develop and implement the campaign, Fischer created the Partnership for a Compassionate Louisville co-chaired by an attorney and Fischer's chief of community building.

Compassionate acts include, for example, shoveling snow for an elderly neighbor or helping a student read. In 2012, the year it was implemented, 90,000 people volunteered for a day of service. According to Fischer, "Earning an international reputation as a city of compassion will help set Louisville apart, identifying our community as a place where people want to live and companies want to locate and grow their business."[8] Here are excerpts from Louisville's extraordinary vision, mission, and value statements:

Vision: A community and world becoming more and more compassionate.

Mission: To champion and nurture the growth of compassion. We ask: "What does compassion want for Louisville?"

Values:

Compassion. This is *the* shared purpose and principle. Compassion is common ground and a unifying force in our polarized world. Compassion impels us to work tirelessly to alleviate the suffering of our fellow creatures . . . to honor the inviolable sanctity of every single human being, treating everybody, without exception, with absolute justice, equity, and respect. Compassion is the bridge between internal practice and external change. . . .

Beauty. Compassion calls for a beautiful morality. It seeks to see the beauty in what is and incorporate the shadow . . .

Inclusion. Anyone and everyone who commits to compassion is welcomed.

Empowerment. This campaign is about empowering people to make a difference in their own life and the lives of others. Compassion is not pity.

Transparency. There is no political agenda. The effort exists . . . to help the citizens of our community reap the benefits that come from living a compassionate life—which are many.

Universally Positive. "The best criticism of the bad is the practice of the better," said St. Francis of Assisi. The effort is solely designed to advance compassionate action . . .

Social Innovation. Individuals and groups are free to embody compassion in their own ways.

Paying It Forward. Anyone who participates "owes" no one anything other than to "pay it forward." People are encouraged to participate simply to experience firsthand the thrill and joy associated with compassionate living.

Hospitality. We will welcome guests in the name of compassion.

Abundance. What we have is enough if we share and if we allow it to flow.

Awareness/Understanding. We strive to keep compassion in our daily thoughts and practice, and to understand the meaning of compassion and its relation to charity, justice, and good works.

Intention. We make a conscious choice to continually grow both our commitment and capacity for compassion.[9]

Impressive, isn't it?

WHAT TO DO WHEN YOUR COMPANY LACKS COMPASSION

But what if you don't work for an organization with heart or for a boss who graduated from Emotional Intelligence 101? What if for financial or other reasons you are not ready to quit?

Instead of being discouraged, shutting down emotionally, or allowing your energy to be depleted, why don't you spread kindness? It's not hard once you recognize that you have more influence than you think. In many organizations, culture change is created one person or one department at a time. Why not in yours? According to Paul Marsden, a social psychologist who studies how ideas spread, "socio-cultural phenomena can spread through, and leap between, populations more like outbreaks of measles or chicken pox than through a process of rational choice."[10] That means positive emotions such as kindness, compassion, and caring can spread through a workplace like a good virus infecting people before they even think about it.

The heart is the body's largest oscillator; sensitive instruments can pick up its electromagnetic field from several feet away. In fact, the heart's field, as measured by an electrocardiogram in one individual, could be detected and measured in another person's brain waves when they touched or were seated in close proximity. As our energetic field changes, as we experience different emotions, the other person picks up these changes. HeartMath research also discovered that the information transmitted by someone who is angry, fearful, depressed, or experiencing other negative emotions takes on beneficial properties when it is influenced by positive emotions such as appreciation, care, and compassion. This implies that *the emotional patterns that underlie stress can be re-patterned by focusing on positive emotions or by being in the presence of someone who is exuding positive emotions*. The result is a dramatic change in heart rhythm and in the neural, hormonal, and biochemical processes that dissipate stress.

Furthermore, research by New York University professor Jonathan Haidt shows that people experience "a warm, uplifting feeling when they see unexpected acts of human goodness, kindness, courage, or compassion." He calls this experience "elevation" because "seeing other people rise on the vertical dimension toward goodness seems to make people feel higher on it themselves. . . . It makes a person want to help others and to become a better person himself or herself."[11]

Thus, it's possible that by giving kindness, caring, compassion, and appreciation to colleagues, they in turn will pass it on, thus shifting the organizational culture. And when that happens, your stress level is bound to go down because the work environment is more user-friendly. As in any social change movement, the first step, as Gandhi pointed out, is to "become the change you want to see."

Here, then, are five transformational ways to make that happen.

Recognize the Different Languages of the Heart

Just as there are different genders, cultures, and languages, there are different ways people express their heartfelt emotions and thoughts:

- For the achiever who gets love through winning, caring may be a pat on the back, a smile, a "job well done."
- For the person who seeks to control in a world perceived as hostile, caring may be an expression of loyalty and protection—full disclosure of information, an agreement with a decision, a willingness to be there in the hard times.
- For the person who needs to be needed, care is recognition, attention, an acknowledgment of who the person is rather than what the person does.

Most of us want to receive the same expressions of the heart that we provide others in order to verify that we are cared for. These expressions are based on our specific worldview and habits of attention. Thus, the more your worldview and particular perspective of caring align with that of your supervisor, coworkers, and the organization as a whole, the more fulfilled you feel at work. When you feel cared for and secure, you are usually willing to treat others in kind.

However, since there are many worldviews and thus different languages of the heart, we may, at times, think we are treating people with care only to find out that they do not perceive it that way. Such was the case with Lisa, a human resources director:

"How I do my work is very detailed," Lisa explained, clasping her hands tightly together. "I arrive at 7:30 and immediately focus on my tasks. I enjoy being alone and get a lot accomplished. I never thought twice about my routine until recently. In an assessment of my leadership style, my employees interpreted my behavior as a sign that I do not care about them. When I found this out, I was shocked. 'What do you want me to do?' I asked them. 'When you arrive at work, do you want me to come out of my office, get a cup of coffee, and chat a bit?' That's exactly what they wanted! So I changed my routine. I now get my coffee, wander through the department, and talk with people for fifteen minutes.

A Seed of Truth

"Nobody cares how much you know until they know how much you care."

—THEODORE ROOSEVELT

They love it! It's not my personality to be chatty. I demonstrate care by meeting with them individually, reviewing their goals, and asking what I can do for them. Clearly, my experience of care and theirs is very different."

Understanding the different languages of the heart is even more complicated than understanding the different personality types. Although there is no data showing that there is any difference between men's and women's innate ability to feel compassion and to empathize, they tend to express compassion and care in different ways because boys and girls have been socialized differently. Add cultural differences to this, and it's amazing that we understand each other's heart at all! If you are uncertain if your coworker cares about you, listening to his words and observing his body language may offer some clues. If you are still unsure, it's time to ask for what you want.

Ask for What You Need

Deana, a human resource director, told me this story:

"My elderly father recently fell. For a time he didn't know where he was and couldn't think logically. Although I have three siblings, only my brother and I live nearby, so we were the ones to help care for him and give my stepmom some time away to re-energize. I ran back and forth to the hospital, but still put in the long hours my job requires. During this time, I was also in the midst of remodeling my kitchen.

"Although I have a group of close friends, it's not my style to ask for support. I realize now that I expected people to be mind readers and to offer support without my asking for it. One day, I received a voice message from a close friend asking about the remodeling, but no mention of my father; I was furious.

"I couldn't decide if I had the right to be angry. I had no blueprint for this kind of experience. I also was shocked that my closest friends were not the ones who were front and center, and that others showed more concern and empathy. I called my brother, a psychologist, for his perspective. He suggested that since we don't know what illness and aging parents conjures up for people, we give them more latitude. I think he's right. I also think it's time for me to start asking for what I want."

After over thirty years coaching executives and their teams, I'm still surprised that, like Deana, many leaders don't ask for what they want. Sure, they can ask for and demand what the business needs, but rarely do I hear them asking for what they emotionally need. Andrew, the owner and CEO of a multimillion-dollar small business, is terrific at caring for and recognizing the accomplishments of his employees, yet he told me that it is extremely rare for an employee to express appreciation for him. "I assume that they think the boss doesn't need it or want it, but in truth I do." "Have you ever told them that or asked for it directly?" I questioned. For all his smarts and emotional sensitivity, he had never thought of it. Perhaps his pride gets in the way.

In a recent assessment of a nonprofit organization's culture, a common concern was *we don't tell each other our feelings or ask for help*. Yet, these same people are excellent at extending care and support to their clients. Although participants expect help from their coworkers and are disappointed when they don't receive it, they rarely directly confront the issue. By saying nothing, they tacitly agree that it is okay not to extend care and support to each other. Thus, to spread care we also need to give and receive feedback in addition to asking for what we want.

Give the Gift of Feedback

Just as the heart radiates an energetic outflow, it also receives energy. This two-beat happens often within the course of a day. Sometimes heartfelt energy is generated from seeing a picture of a loved one, your boss's smile of approval, or an unexpected bonus for a job well done. You receive it, and its positive emanation spreads through you.

At other times, the heart speaks in words, communicating your inner intricacies so others can get to know you; at other times it provides feedback. Feedback is a gift that explains what someone needs from you and what you can do to satisfy that need, and vice versa. You'd think most people would be delighted to receive it. WRONG! Many of us become defensive; perhaps we assume the worst, judge the person offering the feedback (How dare he tell me how to do my job when he always makes mistakes!), or get indignant because someone has standards or expectations for our behavior. Yet, to understand someone else's heart, you need to let go of the judgments and defensiveness and replace them with curiosity. "Isn't that interesting" coupled with "tell me more" serves as a bridge leading to true dialogue.

Yvonne Ginsberg, a consultant and trainer for Google's Search Inside Yourself program, pointed out the following to me:

> "It's not just criticism that produces a reaction in us; praise does as well. Our reaction limits our ability to hear the full communication. Thus, to understand another's heart, we need to learn to quiet our reaction. At Google, they call this 'developing attentional intention.' The first step is to be sensitive to what is going on inside you. Then you need to neutralize it rather than making it the fuel that generates your reaction."

You can do this by taking three deep breaths, re-centering yourself, saying pause and delete to your reaction, or any of the other techniques I've provided that work for you.

Next, thank the person for the feedback, whether you agree with all, some, or none of it. That person took a risk providing feedback when many people would have said nothing and complained behind your back. Look for the seed of truth in the feedback and, when you find it, acknowledge it. You may have a perfectly good reason for doing whatever it is, but the other person can't know it until you share it. You don't have to change your behavior because someone gives you feedback, but you should seriously consider it. If you find making a change will upgrade you as an individual and spread kindness and care, then make the change. Your transformation will tell the person you heard and agreed, and a new level of trust and heartfelt connection will develop. Of course, adding a verbal sprinkle of appreciation also helps.

Make Giving and Receiving Appreciation a Habit

A little appreciation for a person's good qualities or talents has the power to interrupt a stressful or negative experience, redirect a person who's racing through the day to their "home," and remind the person of the next best version of them. Appreciating people at work tells them that you value their contribution and helps them feel safe. As Richard Branson, founder of the Virgin Group, said, "Like flowers flourish on water, people flourish on praise."[12]

Although it's helpful to our well-being, many of us do not freely spread our appreciation. Some are uncomfortable giving praise; it's too touchy-feely. Others are so engrossed in other things that appreciation takes a back burner. Also, as part of our survival mechanism, we as a species are caught up in what psychologists call the "negativity bias." According to Jonathan Haidt,[13] professor of ethical leadership at

NYU, "responses to threats and unpleasantness are faster, stronger, and harder to inhibit than responses to opportunities or pleasures." Thus, when we have relationship difficulties with a colleague, we are often so focused on the negative that, even if we see the positive, we don't mention it. Yet, positive feedback can soften a difficult relationship and even heal it. Furthermore, when we give appreciation often, it becomes a habit, shifting our focus from the negative to the life-affirming positive.

As hard as it is for people to give appreciation, it is even harder for many of us to receive it. Sometimes when I work with teams, I guide them in an appreciation exercise in which one person stands in the middle of the circle and the others offer praise and appreciation. The person in the middle is told to face the speaker and make eye contact while being praised. Instead of beaming in the sunlight of recognition, as you might suppose, people often energetically contract as if they want to get out of the spotlight as quickly as possible.

Perhaps we are so used to focusing on what is wrong with ourselves that we become uncomfortable when we're told what is right. Or maybe we are so used to giving energy, or love for that matter, that we are unpracticed in receiving it. Both giving and receiving heartfelt expression require openness and vulnerability, which are not easy. In the Personal Practice section, you'll find an energy practice to help you train yourself to give and receive heart energy.

Ultimately, appreciation begins at home—by giving it to yourself. It means noticing what's right in you, acknowledging when you exceed your preconceived limits, and recognizing the good intent and energy you contribute, whether or not you succeed. As you develop self-appreciation, you'll notice it becomes easier to spot the goodness, talent, and contributions of others and to praise them for it. Over time, you'll probably notice that others start appreciating you more. This creates a positive energy network, which has the power to unite and elevate people. It's a heck of a stress reducer.

Become Comfortable with Being Vulnerable

Although we may intellectually know that we need to ask for what we want, give feedback, and show appreciation to others and ourselves, doing it is still hard for many of us. In the traditional workplace, personal identity is so often tied to work title, status, and/or paycheck that relationships take a backseat; work is about maintaining power and achieving results in the most efficient manner possible. Often people are viewed solely as commodities. If you work for a self-absorbed boss who is primarily concerned with his or her goals or advancement, it's hard to ask for what you emotionally need. Judith, for example, a senior executive in a tech company, told me that her boss contacted her a day after her sister's funeral to tell her to ask one of her reports to contact several vendors:

> "She could have contacted my subordinate directly. She's interrupted my weekends and my vacations before for unimportant things. Although I've talked with her about setting boundaries and asked that she only call me if things are urgent, she doesn't hear me. She thinks I should be at her beck and call 24/7. I've stopped discussing my needs with her. You'd think she would be more caring particularly because I am very good at my job. I've tried to go with the flow, but this time she stepped way over the line. I'm so stressed and insulted that I'm thinking of quitting, although I love my job."

My first response was to console and agree with Judith. Clearly, her boss was out of line. My second response was to wonder how and why Judith kept herself in the victim role. Sure, she loved her job and wanted to keep it; yes, she tried to negotiate her boundaries. However, when negotiations failed, why didn't she take better care of herself and tell her boss unequivocally "NO MORE"? If her boss couldn't read her subtle

A Seed of Truth

*"Self-absorption in all forms kills empathy,
let alone compassion. The more attentive we are to
others, the more keenly we will sense their inner
state and pick up on subtle cues."*
—DANIEL GOLEMAN

emotional cues, why didn't Judith explain how her boss's behavior was affecting her? Did she really think her boss would fire her? Didn't she understand her professional value? Didn't she value herself? As the eldest of five siblings, was she so used to being responsible and in control that it was hard for her to show vulnerability?

Many of us are afraid to be vulnerable particularly in the workplace. We equate vulnerability with weakness and fear that someone will take advantage and harm us. You may remember Peterson, the brilliant Silicon Valley thinker who kept walking into pillars (see Chapter 3). Once people saw him as vulnerable, he became more approachable. When you are willing to be transparent, declare your feelings, and admit your mistakes, you give permission to others to do the same. The myth of the perfect leader who has all the answers has outlived its time. People trust those with humility, who are engaged in lifelong personal development, and who are willing to enter into dialogue rather than assume they always have the right answer. The Enneagram speaks to our fear of vulnerability. No matter whether it is the Type 1, who is afraid of being wrong, or the Type 3, who is afraid of failing, they have the same concern—the need to feel safe. In the Application for Teams section, there are suggestions for creating agreements to help your team feel safe so they may contribute their best. As for Judith, she begrudgingly took care of her boss's needs and not her own. I call this a rescue.

Learn to Give and to Receive Help

There are three reasons people rescue others. Some rescue because they put others before themselves; for example, they help colleagues with their work, but may not have time for their own. Others rescue because they think they must to keep their jobs. Still others pride themselves on being a hero or fixer. No matter the reason, if you find yourself engaging in one of the following three forms of rescue, it's time to stop and call your attention back:

1. You do something for someone that they want you to do although you don't want to do it.
2. You do something for someone although they don't want you to do it.
3. You do something for someone who doesn't want you to do it, and you don't want to do it.

All of us receive pleasure when we feel that our work has helped someone. Once we recognize that our work is meaningful, it diminishes or puts into perspective the annoyances and frustrations that occur in any job. Yet, giving indiscriminately creates emotional fatigue and stress.

Giving is an art. Instead of continually giving attention to others, use only as much emotional energy as the situation requires, which will help prevent emotional burnout or resentment. Second, know your boundaries and honor them. Get comfortable with saying "no." You don't have to apologize for taking care of yourself. "No" is a full statement. Giving begins with your honoring yourself so you have enough in your emotional bank account to give to others. If you are only skilled at giving, it is time to learn to receive. If you are a receiver, it's time to learn to give. When you can do both, a peaceful kindness revolution occurs, positively transforming the workplace.

Create a Kindness Community

The senior vice president in charge of research and development of a global brand wanted to create his dream team. Although his senior leaders worked well together in crisis, they had petty disagreements and didn't truly understand each other or recognize the others' contributions. I was hired to create an emotionally intelligent collaborative team. For two years, we held quarterly retreats that focused on such topics as shared ownership for change, how to dissent in a way that benefited the team, how to have difficult discussions that led to resolution and understanding, what caring looked like for each of them, and what the difference was between power and force. Members created a Yes . . . AND? Initiative, made team agreements, expanded their collective view on what inclusion looked like, and did some mind/body/energy work.

After two years, the senior vice president and I agreed that the team needed to put their new knowledge into practice, so he created a division-wide innovation initiative. He stepped away and became the initiative's champion. I continued to coach him; the senior leaders took charge as the initiative's sponsors.

The team created experiences for the division with the goals of opening the associates' minds, connecting them, and wowing them. They chose four excellent team leaders and divided the division into four groups. Everyone—chemists, quality control experts, process engineers, and administrators—was involved. As the senior leaders learned to let go of control, something magical happened. Everyone including administrators became idea makers; the workplace became vibrant as people engaged in challenging, meaningful conversations; laughter echoed through the halls. People went out of their way to appreciate and recognize each other. Instead of being competitive and secretive, teams shared suggestions for innovation with other teams. Before we knew it, the workplace transformed into one that not only supported the bottom line by creating a significant number of innovations, but also supported the human spirit. As one person put it, "I never worked harder and I never had as much fun."

When visiting the division, the U.S. company president immediately noticed how different it felt. He was impressed by the high energy and how people treated each other. Later, he brought his executive team to the division for an informal town hall meeting at which they interviewed everyone in the division. None of the responses were scripted. People spoke from their hearts. By the time the meeting ended, it was clear to the executives that nobody does it alone.

Find Meaning and Significance

The story of openhearted connection at work cannot be complete without reference to Google. Compassion is organic there, growing from the bottom up. From its inception, Google's message was that it wanted to do no evil. Because of that intention and because of its highly intellectual image, people who are attracted to working at Google are not only brilliant, they are also idealistic. They want to work with a company that is doing good. According to Google's Yvonne Ginsberg, underlying this idealism are three general assumptions: All people really want to be loving; all people really want to be happy; and all people really want to be in goodness. "If these assumptions underline your communication," she told me, "it speaks directly to the heart and wakes it up while strengthening it within you. In Google we acknowledge that the other person is just like me." This belief is the basis for their one-day focus on compassion taught as part of their Search Inside Yourself program.

This course was developed by engineer Chade-Meng Tan (called Meng) as part of Google's 20 percent factor. Employees are required to spend 20 percent of their time working on projects that have nothing to do with their job descriptions. Meng, whose current job description is to "enlighten minds, open hearts, create world peace," not only co-teaches the program, he wrote a bestselling book based on the class. Other employee-generated programs include raising money to build a hospital in India that serves over 20,000 people. After the Haiti earthquake, engineers and product managers developed a tool that helped earthquake victims find their loved ones. Employees developed each of these without asking for permission. In fact, so much corporate giving comes from the grassroots that two "Googlers" formed the social responsibility team that supports all of these efforts.

At Google, they take the notion of nobody does it alone seriously, spreading streams of goodness, compassion, and care to places that need it the most. It's a wonderful win-win. When people make a difference, they feel significant and their work and lives are filled with meaning. Pressure is exciting and, if stress occurs, it is tolerable because it is in service of something that truly matters.

When you change people's hearts, you change the organizational culture. And when you change the culture, you have a shot at changing the world. Consider the following quotation from Albert Einstein:

Strange is our situation here on earth. Each of us comes for a short visit, not knowing why, yet sometimes seeming to divine a purpose. From the standpoint of daily life, however, there is one thing we know.

We are here for the sake of others. Above all for those upon whose smile and well-being our own happiness depends, and also for the countless unknown souls with whose fate we are connected by a bond of sympathy.

Many times a day I realize how much my own outer and inner life is built upon the labors of my fellow men, both living and dead, and how earnestly I must exert myself in order to give in return as much as I have received.

PERSONAL PRACTICE

AWAKENING THE HEART: GIVING AND RECEIVING HEARTFELT ENERGY

For most of us, the hurts we collect over our lifetime are stuck in our hearts. To protect ourselves from further pain, we've learned to armor our hearts, which makes receiving and/or giving care and love challenging. To open your heart and reestablish a healthy balance between giving and receiving heartfelt energy, you first need to explore your heart's current reality. Here's a practice that will help.

Take a few deep breaths, holding the inhale for a few seconds before breathing out. Let the exhale be longer than the inhale. Let go of control of your breathing; allow the natural circular rhythm to take over. After a short while, you'll notice that your breathing is like a wave. When you feel relaxed, direct your attention and breathe to your heart. It may be easier if you place your hand on it.

Imagine your breath radiating from inside your heart out into the field around you. Can you feel the rise and fall of your chest or is it hardly moving? Does your heart muscle feel tight or armored or does it move freely? Does your heart feel tender or aching? Either way, don't blame yourself or analyze your past. Just concentrate your attention and breathe into your heart and imagine/sense/feel that it is softening. As it does, notice any emotions, no matter how slight. Allow them to build and express themselves. If your heart area seems numb or if you don't think anything is happening, direct your attention into the nothingness and describe it to yourself. The smallest description, no matter how insignificant it may seem, will begin the process of opening your heart. Keep feeling into your heart; allow each sensation to appear. Do thoughts and/or memories arise? If you need to cry, then cry. If you need to rage at the universe, let it out in a safe way. Then bring your attention back into your heart and notice whether it feels more relaxed and softer. You'll find that the more you allow feelings to flow through the heart, the more open you are to joy, truth, and a state of oneness.

The next step is to notice the two-beat energy that radiates from your heart when you exhale, and radiates back when you inhale. How far out do you radiate heart energy? How strong is the current of energy flow both in and out? Imagine that someone you love or care for is standing in front of you. Send loving energy to that person and then sense/feel the person's care and love back into your own heart.

Then, go farther. Instead of just beaming heart energy into the field in front of you, imagine what it would feel like if you were standing in a field of heart energy. Have you noticed that stress doesn't live in this space? In fact, it's just the opposite. As the energy/pressure that moves through your system connects with the larger energy field, the greater your sense of well-being, inner joy, and connection will be. In these moments, you will feel supported and know that you are not alone.

Practice this exercise once a day. If you are too busy for a long practice, take a few minutes before you go to sleep or immediately on rising to feel your heart's energy. Following each practice, ask yourself how much space you sense in your heart. Over the days and weeks of practice, notice whether the sensations change. Is it easier to be in touch with what you feel during the day? Has your level of empathy and compassion changed?

APPLICATION FOR TEAMS

SPREAD KINDNESS AND CONNECTION

How as a leader do you call forth compassion and kindness so it resonates in every person and echoes through the hallways of your organization? How do you encourage interaction and a true feeling of connection among employees so they feel supported and collaborative?

How do you support people so they contribute their best? The process, I have learned, begins with building a base of safety.

Who you are when you feel safe is significantly different from who you are when you feel afraid and/or stressed. When safe, the control-obsessed bosses open their hearts and soften, transforming themselves into caring and helpful advocates for others' success. When safe, the helpers, who habitually empower others' feelings and points of view more than their own, are free to express their creativity and add their voice to the world. When safe, the observers step out of the shadows, connect with others, and assert their feelings, needs, and opinions. When safe, you find the hidden or underutilized qualities, talents, and treasures of your being. In those moments, you affirm yourself and, in so doing, are more willing to treat others with kindness and care.

If you are serious about bringing the heart to work, next Monday morning gather your staff and ask each of them:

- How do they behave when they feel safe? How does their sense of safety affect their relationships, their performance, creativity, collaborations, and their sense of self? Ask other team members to add their observations and experiences to people's self-reflections.
- What helps them feel safe? What do they require from you and from other team members? What more can they, themselves, do to feel safe?
- If everyone on the team were feeling safe, how would this change the team, department, and/or organization? For example, would people interact and help each other more? Would they give each other feedback, ask for what they need, and show appreciation more often? Would these behaviors support the business goals? If so, in what ways?
- At team meetings, would each person agree to discuss when they are not feeling safe and what they need at these times?

Create a weekly ritual in which team members share their preceding week's experiences of kindness and appreciation. Some members will resist. Remind them that the qualities they bring to work determine whether it is fulfilling. Ask for a four-week commitment after which it will be reevaluated. After each weekly meeting, ask members to anonymously respond to the following questions based on the past week.

On a scale of 1 to 10 with 1 being extremely unimportant and 10 being extremely important, rate the following:

1. Did acts of caring and kindness affect your job satisfaction?

2. Did you learn anything about bringing your heart to work?

3. Did the emphasis on kindness affect the team's performance and interactions?

Notice at the end of the four weeks whether members' understanding of kindness has expanded and whether they are more willing to engage in these conversations. Feed these results back to the team.

NINE

SPARK CREATIVE SOLUTIONS IN HIGH-PRESSURE SITUATIONS

Listening Is More Than Hearing

The most exciting breakthrough of the 21st century will occur not because of technology but because of an expanding concept of what it means to be human.

—John Naisbett, *Megatrends 2000*

Back in the 1970s, when I was twenty-three, I lived for a couple of months on Formentera, a small Spanish island in the Mediterranean. There I met Cindy, who traveled with me to Morocco. For a number of reasons, including the desire to meet Moroccans, we ended up traveling third class on the night coach from Fez to Casablanca. We had no idea at the time that this train was one of the most infamous in the world.

The third class coach's wooden benches accommodated four people. Every two rows of benches faced each other. Unlike American trains, there was no conductor, dining car, or other amenities. We quickly realized that we were the only two women in that car, which was crowded with boisterous young men. We promised each other to remain vigilant during the eight-hour train ride.

It didn't take long before the men decided we were the entertainment for the night and tried to engage us. They sat so close to us that we were pushed to the other side of the benches. When Cindy and I fled into another compartment, they followed, cheering and calling after us. One was a military man who spoke English. I hoped he might translate what we said and protect us; he didn't. He didn't harass us, but he seemed to enjoy watching the others do so. No one else on the train came to our aid.

Hours passed and the tension mounted. Verbal intimidation was followed by touching—our faces, arms, legs, backs, and especially Cindy's long blond hair. I watched as tears streamed down her cheeks. I wasn't much better; stressed and afraid, I felt like a trapped animal. I sensed my attention locate outside of me and into every move of our tormentors. My legs felt frozen and my mind raced. I feared rape or murder. I imagined they would throw my body off the train and that my parents would never know what happened to me. However, when the ringleader, far taller and obviously stronger, grabbed me, something within me shifted. I sensed my attention being drawn back deeply inside me. My mind quieted and my mind/body knew exactly what to do. Although I had never hit anyone before, I smacked him as hard as I could across the face. For a moment, he hesitated. Then he picked me up, laid me down on a bench, and stood guard over me for the rest of the trip. I urged Cindy to do the same, but she was unable to, and they continued taunting her.

When we reached Casablanca the next morning, the military man told me that the ringleader wanted to marry me. He explained that from their point of view, women traveling alone at night, particularly in third class, were either nuns or whores. As we were clearly not nuns, they assumed the worst. When I smacked him, it changed the ringleader's perception of me. From that night on, I understood the power of my intuition in guiding me through high-pressure situations.

All of us have experienced flashes of intuition. Yet, few of us know how to invite these moments into our lives so they occur more consistently. In the absence of answers to our challenges, we worry like the alcoholic who went from being late for work to concluding he was going to lose his job and family. Worry creates a continuous loop of doom and gloom and, more times than not, it's time and energy spent unproductively.

Although the last thing we want to hear when we are up to our neck in problems is that they may be blessings in disguise, it is true not only because we learn from them, but also because the pressure has the power to transform. Think of Nelson Mandela and the twenty-seven years he spent in prison. That experience changed him from what some called a terrorist to an extraordinary man of forgiveness and peace.

Similarly, once we learn how to open and align to the energy in our mind/body field, pressure broadens our perspective and increases options by enhancing our perceptions. Intuition, or gut feeling, becomes more available and dreams that offer guidance are clearer and more frequent. We notice the details and patterns and spot the connections between things more easily. As our perceptions heighten, creative solutions appear. We recognize that we are not merely responders to life; *we are creators*. Thus, instead of increased pressure resulting in stress, pressure becomes the key to a richer, more exciting, and connected life.

This chapter focuses on sparking creative solutions to high-pressure situations through intuition, dreams, living in the question, and shifting brain wave patterns to open to what Jung called the "collective unconscious," a place where all ideas already exist. The journey begins with listening, but not in the way we habitually listen, which is to say, listening is more than hearing.

HOW TRULY LISTENING CAN CHANGE YOUR LIFE

As Richard Moon, founder of extraordinarylistening.com, told me, "Hearing is knowing what someone said, while listening implies opening our minds to grow and change because of the input. Let me explain it this way. There were many things my parents told me when I was a kid. I heard them. I just didn't listen."

The difference between hearing and listening is attention. Where we locate our attention—what we choose to listen to—has the power to change our lives. The more willing we are to be changed by what we receive, the more open we are to considering it, and the more likely we are to perceive a truer reality than if we allow in only certain information.

Yet, most of us are too distracted, smug, or insecure to listen attentively. We interrupt, judge, and tune out, particularly when the person's point of view is different from ours. Most of us listen with an agenda, particularly at work. We want what we want and in the workplace, which many consider unsafe, we listen to that which can either hinder or help us advance our interests.

However, true listening occurs when we are receptive, when we don't expect or want anything. It requires temporarily giving up control so we can allow not only the spoken words, but also the sound of the voice and the emotions to resonate. Quicker than any other sense, listening tunes our brain to the patterns of our environment.[1] It acts as an alarm system to help us survive, and it enhances our intellectual acuity. As every artist, inventor, or scientist knows, listening is not about forcing order on the creative or problem solving process, but about attending so sensitively that we get out of the way and allow answers to be revealed in their own time. However, before we can listen deeply to someone, we need to be able to listen to ourselves.

The Partnership of the Rational and Intuitive Minds

Allison, the CEO of a nonprofit agency, told me:

> "Every year a national insurance company holds a large event in my county. The highlight of the event is a lottery drawing in which the company dispenses funds to nonprofit organizations. The only requirements are that you have to be at the event and, if your name is called, you have only ten minutes to claim your prize. Before I went, I asked a trusted staff member to check the logistics

to ensure we would hear our name if we won. At the event, despite assurances, I couldn't shake the feeling that we weren't seated in the correct place. I was right; they called our name, and we didn't hear it. We lost $10,000 because I didn't trust my intuition."

Many of us ignore our intuition and rely primarily on our logic and experience. However, the rational mind, which enables us to recall facts and experience, analyze, and synthesize, can be limiting, particularly in an information-glutted society where collecting all the data may not be possible when quick decisions are needed. In addition, we may, at times, twist our facts to fit our theories or, when faced with a pressing problem, fail to notice important details because we panic or rush. At other times, we assume conventional wisdom or past solutions can fit today's problem, but that isn't necessarily so. For example, Paul McCartney has said that when he and John Lennon wrote, they tried never to repeat the same formula. Instead, they would change the system and pattern in order to write something different.[2]

Unlike McCartney and Lennon, many of us relegate our inquisitiveness to the attic of our minds as we go round and round in the same old ways. Faced with the infinite universe, we are compelled to create stories to describe to ourselves what we perceive. Once we connect the dots in a particular way, it becomes more difficult to see them another way; yet, often, we don't see all the dots right away. The complexity of our world demands that we examine each challenge from a deeper place with a fresh perspective. By focusing on the roots of the issue, we uncover its secrets and reveal its ripple effects. By going beneath the surface, we tap into our intuition and *understand* our problem more completely.

The Role Listening to Intuition Plays

Intuition is the process of perceiving or knowing things to a high degree of certainty without conscious reasoning. Albert Einstein said it was "the highest form of knowing." Through intuition we sense what the

A Seed of Truth

"The intuitive mind is a sacred gift and the rational mind is a faithful servant. We have created a society that honors the servant and has forgotten the gift."
—ALBERT EINSTEIN, Physicist and Nobel Laureate

eyes do not see and the ears do not hear. Bursts of inner knowing come to us quickly and are hard to shake. If we keep an open mind, intuition can provide solutions to problems or decisions that we hadn't perceived.

Intuition delivers information from our unconscious minds and affects our psycho-physiological system, thus bringing emotions and sensations along with our "aha" moments. Michael Eisner, former CEO of Walt Disney Company, says that when he hears a good idea, his body often reacts in a certain way—he sometimes gets an unusual feeling in his stomach, throat, or on his skin. "The sensation is like looking at a great piece of art for the first time," he said.[3]

Over the years, studies have shown that leaders often rely on their intuition to solve complex problems when logical methods are not sufficient. In fact, the higher up the ladder, the more leaders use intuition as their inner guidance system. This ability differentiates them from middle managers. Intuition is often the difference between business as usual and a true leap forward. For example, Google's self-driving car project, led by Sebastian Thrun, a Google fellow and Stanford professor, is an example of inner knowing. Well before all the necessary information, maps, and infrastructure were available, Thrun intuited that self-driving cars were possible. Motivated in part by the death of a friend in a traffic accident, he formed a team to address the problem at Stanford without knowing what he was doing.[4]

Think of the moments when you didn't know what you were doing, yet that magic message found you anyway. It may have been as simple as sensing that your boss, with the open door policy, didn't want to be disturbed or as complex as making quick decisions in a war zone under enemy fire. For author and teacher Richard Daffner, the magic message came when he was hiking in the Himalayas. He'd spent the night in an isolated chai shop (a primitive mud structure at approximately 14,000 feet). He hiked to 17,000 feet to see the factory in which monks made cheese, and then continued further up the mountain. Suddenly, he spotted a cloud. The sky was still blue, but an alarm went off inside him. Richard turned, began hiking quickly, then running down the mountain. When he reached the chai shop, there were two or three inches of snow on the ground. The next morning, there were two feet of snow. Had he stayed longer he might not have made it back down.

Researchers suggest that when we use our intuition, we draw on patterns or cues that come from our experience and are stored in our subconscious mind. Thus, an expert's intuition tends to be more reliable than that of a rookie. Furthermore, the wider your knowledge base, the greater the possibility of pattern recognition. However, the scientific instruments used to understand and record our senses, while better than they were, often are unable to show the whole picture. Yet, science recognizes that when intuition occurs, our brain waves' frequencies change, which enables us to operate spontaneously from a different and finer state of consciousness.

INCREASE YOUR BRAIN WAVE VIBRATION, STIMULATE YOUR INTUITIVE POWER

Imagine you are in your usual work mode juggling a number of projects, considering options, making decisions, and running from meeting to meeting. You may be dragging your tail or in a heightened state of alertness. Either way, you are operating in a beta state of mind—normal waking consciousness, which includes reasoning—where your brain wave frequency ranges from 14 to 40 Hz (cycles per second). Assume that your colleague, Jack, is concerned about your decision to centralize customer care and passionately suggests another approach. You consider it but decide that your way is best. When he leaves, you notice you feel tense and off-center. In terms of brain activity, you're now in a beta blitz. Researchers tell us that beta brain waves, particularly in higher ranges, may cause self-criticism, anxiety, restlessness, and stress.

When you come home, you take a long hot shower and feel your mind and body relax. Suddenly you realize that Jack's solution is not only good, it rocks. You lie down with your eyes closed, and, as your breath comes in relaxed waves, you suddenly know how to implement Jack's idea in ways that neither of you had considered. You have entered an alpha state in which your brain waves are vibrating at a frequency of 7.5 to 14 Hz. This is the gateway to your subconscious mind. It's a relaxed state, which generates intuition. It occurs naturally during daydreams or light meditation, and provides an opportunity to program your mind, visualize, and imagine.

In a sixteen-year study by Idea Champions, only 3 percent of the 10,000 people interviewed said they had their best ideas at work. The rest had them while walking in nature, on vacation, meditating, and, yes, in the shower.[5] In these unstructured environments, you are not distracted and your attention is in your mind/body—you are relaxed, balanced, and open.

Satisfied and feeling good, you sit down to meditate. After a while, your attention drops deep into your body and then into the field around you. As your body relaxes, you feel spacious and free. The frequency of your brain waves slows to 4 to 7.5 Hz, the theta state, in which you have access to your deepest mental programming and from which great inspiration, extraordinary creativity, and exceptional insight manifest. Rising from your meditation, you know the nuances of how the new model will affect other departments, and give you an unseen edge in the marketplace. You also recognize that your initial decision to centralize customer service was not just a neutral business decision, it was driven by your deep-seated need for control and your fear of vulnerability.

When you consider the many layers of consciousness, you begin to see what entrepreneur and student of meditation Mark Bass pointed out to me:

> "Intuition is the tip of the iceberg. It's the part you see. Below are the unseen gears of life coming together in perfect harmony. Moreover, because they come together in perfect harmony things happen perfectly. You just have to watch for the iceberg. That's the recognition that life is unfolding. The solution will always present itself if you look for it and don't get distracted. Everyone has had that experience."

The challenge is how to invite these insightful "accidents" into your life so they happen more consistently. The journey begins with practice.

PRACTICE, PRACTICE, PRACTICE

General Charles C. Krulak wrote in the *Marine Corps Gazette* that it was imperative for marines to develop their intuitive decision-making skills:

> In short, we must make intuitive decision-making an instinct, and this can only be accomplished through repetition. Training programs and curriculums should routinely make our Marines decide a course of action under cold, wet, noisy conditions while they are tired and hungry and as an instructor continuously asks them *what are you going to do now Marine?*[6]

Faced with numerous tactical challenges, often within the span of a few hours, marines and their leaders need to make the right decision quickly under extreme duress. While most of us will not experience what marines may encounter, you can begin developing your intuitive muscle by practicing in simple ways.

Stephen Samuels, an artist, author, and teacher of meditative practices, told me:

A Seed of Truth

*"Uncertainty is an uncomfortable position
but certainty is an absurd one."*
—VOLTAIRE

"It was summer and I was outside fixing my car. The grass had grown tall, so tall that I couldn't see the ground. Realizing that I needed a certain size block of wood, I was about to go to my shop where I knew I had one, when I was drawn to a certain spot under a tree. On an instinct, I walked over to it and there on the ground was the perfect block of wood for my purpose. Things like that happen often because I don't wait for the big issues to practice using my intuition. For example, I vary my driving routes in accordance with my intuition. When I hear on the news that by taking the back roads, which is usually the longer route, I avoided being stuck on the highway for hours because of an accident, I know my intuition is working."

Small steps can lead to big change.

STOP DOING; START LISTENING

So there you are in the midst of a stressful situation that you can't seem to get a handle on let alone resolve. You've thought it through countless times, tried retrofitting solutions onto the problem, and received lots of well-intentioned advice. Yet, you've gotten nowhere. As is often true for all of us, you don't know what you don't know, which complicates the matter. The good news is that life has provided you with the perfect opportunity to shift your problem-solving approach from doing to listening; from making it happen to living in the question. However, this requires that you suspend any mistrust you have of the unknown and let the sage inside lead you.

The process begins with framing the question. This is important because if you don't have it on your radar screen, if you are not looking for it, it's either not going to show up or you won't notice it when it does. Stephen Samuels shared this:

"One of the things I found that works very well for me, is not to just let the problem run around in my head but to say it out loud in a question form a few times and listen to myself say it. I state the problem every way I can. This process helps me zero in what I am really asking. The first few times I say it I may get nothing, but the third or fourth time I go aha!"

Next, embrace the experience of being lost or confused. Being lost or confused isn't a bad thing; it is just the nature of the journey. If you get uptight and/or try to force your will, you'll energetically contract and close the door to the most creative and revolutionary ideas.

You also need to quiet your ego's demand for concrete comprehensive answers. Instead, move through your problem-solving journey with the same ease and inquisitiveness you had as a child. Just as when you are lost in the woods, your job is to spot the clues so you can find the way out of your dilemma.

Although we are used to thinking linearly, the process of living in the question is more like a treasure hunt. The clues come in their own time and in their own way. You may be sitting in a noisy café and overhear a conversation between people sitting two tables away and that provides the magic message. Or you may be drawn to open a book that you haven't looked at for years, only to find a line that speaks directly to your situation. As in a treasure hunt, where one clue sends you to the next, your conscious mind may think, *that doesn't make any sense*. However, when you reach the destination, you realize you see things differently now.

Sometimes it takes a while to spot clues. Don't give up. At other times, you've collected clues and think you know the answer, only to discover it doesn't work. Don't give up. Often, people will try to discourage you, tell you it's impossible; don't give up.

Jeff, an entrepreneur, confided this:

"Two and a half years ago, I was at the lowest period of my life. I was struggling to raise money for my start-up business but hadn't found any investors. I had no money in my savings account and had just sold my last big asset. I was literally in tears. I wanted to crawl up in a ball and not get out of bed, but I knew I couldn't.

"I heard there was an investor conference at a local hotel. I didn't feel like going, but something inside me said, *go—you never know whom you are going to meet.*

"The first day is a disaster although I do strike up a conversation with a guy named Dave from Massachusetts. He is a little rough around the edges. He seems to know a lot of people, but they don't seem taken to him. Dave seems to be one of those people who don't conform to society's expectations, but he appears to be a good-hearted and decent person.

"After the conference, it takes six tries before we get together and meet at my office. I had a lot going on then and kept making excuses. I didn't see the point. One day, Dave calls; he's in the area, so I say come on over. I'm still trying to raise money; Dave was trying to make it in the brokerage business. I introduce him to people, and he says if he runs into anyone that could help me, he'll send them my way.

"Eight months go by; I don't see or hear from Dave. Then he calls to tell me about George. He doesn't think George has any money, but thinks he has some good ideas about my type of business. We meet; George has some great ideas. I tell him that I didn't want to waste his time talking about new ideas when what I really needed was money. We met on Saturday; on Monday he calls and tells me he has $100,000 he wants to invest in my com-

A Seed of Truth

"If at first the idea is not absurd,
then there will be no hope for it."
—ALBERT EINSTEIN

pany. I was shocked. I had never expected money from George; Dave said he didn't have any.

"If I hadn't gone to the conference and met with Dave, I would never have met George. Because of George, other investors have lined up. My business wouldn't be what it is today without him. The bottom line is that if I hadn't listened to my intuition, none of this would have happened."

Shake Things Up

To allow the big creative idea to emerge, you need to break the shackles that are restraining you. Next are some ideas that may help. In the beginning, you may hear a little voice in your head saying, *this is stupid. It won't work*. Don't give that voice power and don't try to fight it. Instead, say, *yes, you are probably right, but I am going to do it anyway*. Listen to that; then see what happens.

* Recognize any emotional bias that is distorting your intuition. If you are not sure, make a case for both sides. Say them aloud so you can hear yourself. Does any tension arise in your body? That's a clue.
* Talk about your problem with people in other disciplines and with different personality types. Because they habitually listen to different things than you do, they may provide a different perspective.

- Take naps.
- Meditate, take walks in nature, hang out in silence, play with your pets and children, lie on the grass, etc.
- When you wake, set your intention to discover at least one clue each day.
- Ask yourself, *if I were on the other side of this problem, what would I be feeling?* Then allow yourself to spend the day in that feeling.
- Ask yourself how the person you most admire would handle the problem; assume his or her attitude and presence.
- Program your dreams to receive inspiration.

Listen to Your Dreams

Pressed financially, Joachim, a Carmel art gallery owner, needed to expand his business. An additional location would allow him to recycle his inventory and develop a larger customer base. Though Joachim conferred with colleagues and read a great deal about a number of upscale towns, he was unsure which would best suit his needs. He decided to visit each town. Two nights before his first trip, Joachim had a dream in which he saw his new gallery, the street it was on, and the adjacent structures. When he drove through La Jolla, the first town on his list, he quickly found the building he had seen in his dream. He knew he'd found the right place.

When answers come as clear as a bell, it's almost like magic. However, most of our dreams speak to us in symbols that we need to decode to reveal their meaning. Dreams reflect back to us our current mental/emotional/physical/energetic state. They offer us a look at the version of ourselves that is wrestling with the problem and then propose an answer. Sometimes that answer tells us who we are becoming.

There are many different types of dreams: Some just remove the clutter that has accumulated during the day; others predict future events; still others provide universal truths. For our purposes, we will focus on those dreams that teach and help us solve problems so we feel less stress.

Most dreams have three parts. The first provides a time reference. For example, if you dream you are in your childhood bedroom, it is telling you that the issue is a deep-seated one. The second part of the dream lays out the problem as it is occurring currently in your life. The third part provides a solution or tells you how to move past the internal blocks that are holding you back.

Take the case of Jessica, who, after nineteen years of marriage, was beginning to recognize and articulate the deep unhappiness she felt in her marriage. She had adored her husband and for years usually went along with whatever adventure or dream he pursued although that often left them in financial trouble. Now, Jessica was burned-out. Concerned for her own future and that of their daughter, she had spent the last few years learning the financial planning business, and now was setting out to open her own shop with a couple of her former colleagues. Although she was excited about this prospect, she was uncertain and scared.

Jessica had just turned forty when she had this dream:

"I am sleeping in a 'dormitory' type room. We are being observed by a dark-haired lady in a long bathrobe. I don't look at her while she speaks. I focus on sheets of cancelled stamps that seem to represent something about her—where she's been and what she's interested in.

"I am lying between two girls, limbs intertwined though I often try to disentangle myself. On my left is a dark-haired girl who is trusting and childlike, a bit immature, and clinging. On my right is a dark-haired girl who is slightly older, somewhat angry, confrontational, and at times conciliatory. I am older than they are, and am alternately trying to ignore them and include them. I really wish to be rid of them. While the woman talks, I pretend to sleep so I won't have to participate.

"The girls and I are a unit of some sort. It is hard to sleep with all those tangled limbs. The girl on the right finally suggests that she should slide down and sleep crossways to fit better. In the morning, I get up and go to find coffee. A lecture is beginning and the coffee is down the hall in the 'operating room.'"

After discussing this dream with Jessica, here's what she learned from it:

The setting tells her that this is a teaching dream. (She is in a school dormitory.) She looks at the cancelled stamps, which are like passbook stamps, which tells us she is reviewing her life. The woman in the long bathrobe who is observing her is more sophisticated and has more authority. Jessica tells me she doesn't want to make eye contact with her because she is scared, overwhelmed, and wants to be invisible. (She doesn't want to show up.) Jessica is a Type 1 and doesn't want the woman to see her flaws, fearing her judgment. The woman in the robe is also another aspect of Jessica. (She is judging herself.)

In the image of the tangled limbs, the trusting childlike girl on the left is the Jessica who goes along with her husband's financial irresponsibility. The anger of the girl on the right is actually Jessica's power, which is beginning to emerge. She will help Jessica in her fledgling business and in setting boundaries with her husband. Meanwhile, the Jessica in the middle is trying to harmoniously integrate the childlike qualities and her power.

The powerful girl on the right offers the solution. To better fit together, she is going to slide down by their feet and lay crosswise. (Her power will be the foundation or ground for the unit that is Jessica.) In the morning, there is a lecture (more teaching) in the operating room, which represents healing.

The insights of Jessica's dream were the seeds that changed her life radically. She began to trust herself more, judge herself less, and continue to develop her power both in business and personally. After a couple of years in her business, she was offered a key position in a bank, which she took, later rising up the ranks to executive status. She left her husband, and today is happily married to a man whose values match hers.

Program Your Dreams

Before you go to sleep, put a pen and paper on your nightstand so you can write your dreams down when you wake. Then, sit at the edge of your bed and take some deep relaxing breaths. You may even want to meditate. Once you are in a relaxed state, review the problem in your mind. Think about all the people, parts, relationships, etc., involved. Feel into the problem as you mentally review it. Then say aloud, "I am going to have and remember a dream tonight that will provide information about my problem and show me how to best deal with it. The problem concerns . . . (briefly describe it as objectively as possible). I will now have this dream and remember it. I am open to the highest possible insight and guidance."

Don't just say the words. Instead, while you are speaking, feel the power, clarity, and emotion of your intent. Speak from your center/ ground. Then go to sleep. When you awake, write down everything you can remember including your general sense of the dream and your feelings, impressions, images, and any details you remember. You may get up with a solution or find the answer later in the day when something triggers your memory of the dream. If you don't have a dream or can't seem to figure it out, don't worry. Just keep programming your mind at night that you will have and remember a dream that will provide you with the answer and guidance you need.

Here are some dreaming tips:

- Don't try programming dreams when you've been drinking or have gone to sleep having just eaten a large meal; they will interfere with the dream.

- Write down the dream immediately upon waking or you will forget it. Until you're well practiced, you haven't built a clear enough bridge between the waking world and the dream state.

- Ask yourself if you are open to hearing the answer or if you have a preconceived idea of the answer. Are you afraid of hearing the answer because it may mean that you need to quit your job or shake up your life in a major way? The universe is responsive, but you need to ask in an honest way.

- If you are not sure what the symbols or images mean, become them in the present. For example, if you are standing in a large old house whose windows are boarded up, become the house. Say aloud, "I am large and old." Old doesn't necessarily mean elderly; it may mean that you are an "old soul." Then say, "My windows are closed," and feel into it. Are you closed? What don't you allow yourself to see? How does having your windows closed serve you? At first, it may not seem that it does, yet there is a reason you chose closed windows, although that reason may no longer serve you.

You created each of the symbols so they all have meaning. There are books that provide dream symbol interpretations, but remember, you are the leading expert on your dreams. If a symbol doesn't feel right to you, it isn't. Listen to your intuition and trust it.

TO FIND SOLUTIONS, LISTEN TO ALL THE MIND/BODY CLUES

No matter how solutions appear—be they through dreams, intuition, or just living in the question—a centered/grounded state optimizes their occurrence. This is what martial arts instructor Richard Moon told me:

"Just as the clarity of the music comes together when the different sounds within the symphony play together in key, we are best positioned to listen to ourselves when the forces in our own system come together. An inner stillness, an emptiness, a void, a non-doing allows the forces to unite and produce the overall effect of the symphony. It's listening to the music of our own being and the universe as we experience it that guides us to what we really should be doing. It creates the authenticity that most of us seek."

When this occurs, we not only stress less and achieve more; we live our destiny in spite of ourselves.

MEDITATION

The case for meditation has been made and made again. Research shows that it reduces stress, lowers blood pressure, reduces anxiety, and improves mood. It decreases the risk of chronic disease and improves mental clarity and the ability to focus. Meditation enhances compassion, decision-making ability, and memory recall. And, if that isn't enough, it enhances creativity.

The practice is simple. First, choose a chair or mat that you will use whenever you meditate. After you've been meditating for a while, you'll notice the chair or mat triggers a calm state. If you can, set a time to meditate daily, so it becomes a habit.

In mindfulness meditation, which is derived from Buddhist meditation, students are taught to concentrate on breathing into their *hara*, observing each inhale and exhale. When a thought arises, they are instructed not to hold on to it or to follow the thought, but to let it go and return their attention to their breathing. In some meditation practices, students are told to count their breaths until they get to the fourth breath and then to start again at one. Try it for a couple of minutes and you'll see it is more difficult than you think. Many people who try meditation say they failed because they couldn't stop their thoughts. I tell them not to worry; you're not supposed to stop them. It is the nature of the mind to have thoughts.

Meditation teaches two things. First, it helps you notice how your mind works. As you focus within, you observe how thoughts keep emerging and how you automatically follow them as if they were the Holy Grail. Second, it builds a muscle for focusing your attention. After a while, it gets easier to concentrate on your breath and to return your attention to it when you get distracted. Although you may think not much happened during meditation, you will notice when you finish that you feel more relaxed.

If you want to take a leap forward in your meditation practice, I suggest you begin with the inner map. Here's how:

1. **Focus your attention and breathe in your *hara,*** which is just a few inches below your lower belly. Feel the breath expand your lower back and then your rib cage. Let your exhale be longer than your inhale. Drop your jaw and let your tongue lightly touch the upper palate of your mouth. Let your hands form a circle and place them around your *hara*.

2. **Sense/feel your center.** Let your eyes rest in their sockets. Imagine/sense/feel a beam of light the width of a basketball moving through the crown of your head and down through your body into the ground. We will call this "center." Notice how far down your body it goes. Notice how well your physical body, which includes your head, is aligned to this vertical center. If you sense your body is either in front of or behind center, let go of your resistance and allow yourself to gently move into center.

   a. Notice how much space you feel in front of you—how far your energy field projects. Now sense/feel how far your energy field projects in the back: your head, spine, and legs. Allow the muscles to soften. It may feel as if something in the back, which you can let go of, is supporting you.

   b. Sense/feel from the center out through the right side of your body and into the field beyond. Let go of the tension and allow your energy to flow and spread wide. Remember, there are no boundaries except that which you self-impose.

   c. Now do the same with the left side of your body.

3. **Sense/feel your hands.** Let the tensions run out of your shoulders and arms allowing the energy to move through your palms and out your fingers. Imagine your fingers are growing longer. What do you notice now in your hands as they become more present?

4. **Feel your thighs and buttocks on the chair.** Let go of gravity, allowing your body to sink and merge with the chair. Let the energy run down the front and back of your legs like water running through a hose. Sense/feel the energy moving into your feet. Allow your feet to grow wider and longer as you let go of your tensions and become more present. Feel the bottoms of your feet. Sense/feel the roots growing from your feet into the ground. Notice the roots widening and deeply spreading 360 degrees around you.

Now that you are centered, grounded, and open, **refocus your attention and breaths into your *hara*.** When you get to four, begin again at one. At first, it may seem like a lot to do. After a while, it will become part of you and you'll move through it quickly. Your mind will naturally slow down and the moment expands. Of course, this can happen just by counting your breath without taking the time to center or ground yourself; however, embodying your attention will ultimately provide a shortcut to deeper meditation.

5. **Going Deeper.** Once you are present, imagine/sense/feel that you are in a swimming pool. Pull the plug at the bottom of the pool and allow yourself to be drawn through it to the other side. Alternatively, imagine you are in the ocean and sense/feel yourself submerge under the waves to the ocean's floor. Then go beneath the ocean's floor. If you are playing the game, you'll notice a stillness and silence that engulfs you.

6. **Meditation for Inquiry.** Once your attention is in your mind/body/ energy field, pose a question before meditating. Feel into the question, allowing your energy to align to it. Then let it go. People use this method for solving work or personal issues as well as larger spiritual ones. Don't be surprised if the universe responds and an answer appears immediately or within the days that follow.

APPLICATION FOR TEAMS

CREATING A WORKPLACE THAT SUPPORTS
DEEP INNER LISTENING

Before we make changes to the structure of our workplaces and meetings, it's important to look at the culture and how average employees perceive their identity within the organization. First, most people believe that they are valued primarily for what they do: meaning, their ability to complete tasks. This keeps them on a fast track that permits little, if any, time for deep inner listening.

Second, in most meetings, those who talk a lot or whose expertise confers authority, title, or seniority shape the meeting. If someone dissents or wants to have a different conversation, others may perceive the action as unacceptable. It takes a courageous and committed individual to be willing to suggest something different from the party line. Thus, people may think it pointless to delve inside oneself in order to find deeper truths or conclude that it's easier to just get through the meeting so they can move on to the next.

Of course, most companies talk about innovation; in technology and R&D departments, this is a priority. Yet, the push for innovation may be contrary to the group's general culture, which is more about structure and task delivery than inspiration and flow. If you really want people to take the time to listen deeply, you must be willing to shift the way teams and organizations are governed and structured. You need to bring the hidden conversations that people have in private to the table. A good start is to ask members to write down the conversation that the team or community needs to have but is avoiding or unaware of.

In February 2014, Zappos announced it was experimenting with eliminating traditional managerial positions, job titles, and the typical corporate hierarchy in order to break the bureaucratic rigidity and enhance adaptability. It's too early to tell whether this is the wave of the future and whether or not it will lead to deeper listening, conversations that matter, and innovation. However, what all of us can begin immediately to do is to create a work community based on shared ownership for the greater good. That means that as citizens of our community, we get to keep and express our voice. It implies that every person is a contributor and that all ideas are welcome. The shared ownership approach that Peter Block discusses in his book *Stewardship* rests on the premise that the collective wisdom of the group is essential to moving forward. If I know that my point of view is welcome and truly heard, there's a good chance I will spend more time in inner listening. With shared ownership as the community or team's foundation, here are some other approaches to promote inner listening.

- **Use the power of silence.** Beginning the meeting with a moment of silence helps people let go of previous meetings and concerns and become present in the now. A moment of silence also helps shift the nature of the team's conversation from debate to dialogue. As the team settles into silence, they tend to become more relaxed and centered. This collective state of mind helps those who are more distracted and stressed to calm themselves and focus their attention.

- **Try the ten-second rule.** Agree that in a conversation ten seconds will pass before the next person speaks. That provides time for people to listen and feel within themselves before responding.

- **Bring attention to the body.** Before you begin the meeting, ask people to take a moment and check to see if they are balanced on both of their sitting bones or are leaning on one. Bringing the attention into the body allows people to listen and focus more clearly.

- **Use a talking stick during team meetings.** A Native American tradition, it is used during community meetings to help people speak from their hearts and to help listeners pay attention. The person who has the talking stick has the right to speak. When he is done, the stick is passed to the next member of the community who wants to speak.

- **Breathe.** Such a simple thing and yet you'd be amazed at how many people hold their breath. As high performance is associated with an attentive yet relaxed state, it makes sense at the start of the meeting to help people relax. Even better than telling people to take a couple of deep breaths is to guide them in breathing. I ask them to inhale to a count of four, hold it for three, and then exhale to a count of seven. The longer exhale produces a relaxed feeling. I count out loud so the whole team gets in sync.

- **Promote inner listening times.** Encourage people to get away from their desks and take a walk or lie down in nature. Make it fun. Create signs that say OUT TO LISTEN or posters that say HAVE YOU LISTENED TO YOURSELF TODAY?

- **Create meditation rooms and mind/body classes** such as yoga, aikido, and tai chi where people can individually or collectively turn off and tune in. A long list of companies already doing this includes General Mills, Target, Google, and First Direct, so it shouldn't be too hard a sell to the decision makers in your organization.

YOU REACH YOUR DESTINY
IN SPITE OF YOURSELF

What is happiness but the simple harmony between a man and the life he leads?

— Albert Camus

n October 2012, watercolor artist Liora Davis was listening to NPR in her car when she heard a program entitled "In a Tanzanian Village, Elephant Poachers Thrive." The program shed light on the severity of poaching in Africa. Since the cost of ivory skyrocketed, organized crime and terrorist groups have joined local poachers in killing elephants. Last year alone, over 35,000 elephants were brutally slain (entire families with babies and pregnant females). Although experts differ in their opinion, estimates are that if it continues at this rate, African elephants could be extinct in between 10 and 100 years.

The interviewer spoke first to a poacher who explained that there is no work where he lives. Killing an elephant feeds his family for a month. Although Liora was deeply upset, she could understand the man's dilemma. Then the interviewer spoke to another poacher. She asked him if he was aware that elephants mourn. In fact, when an elephant is killed, another elephant—perhaps its mate, baby, or another member of the herd runs to the dead one's side and, while wailing in grief, touches it. "That's true," the poacher laughed. "So when the other elephant comes to touch it, I shoot that one. Then more come and I get to kill them all. It's like a party for me." Hearing that, Liora immediately fell into a state of despair. "If that's the way human beings are," she said to herself, "I'm not sure if I want to be here anymore."

Liora was inconsolable that night. In the morning, as was her practice, she sat in meditation. As her mind quieted, images of elephants appeared. She knew then, without a shadow of a doubt, that she needed to paint them. Although the sadness was still there, she had tremendous energy to move forward with her new art project and started painting immediately.[1]

That day she contacted an organization to ask for permission to use their elephant photos for her paintings. She was told someone would get back to her, but no one did. That didn't stop her though from painting. The seeds of her destiny had been planted many years before.

In 2000, while Liora was living in Nice, France, she participated in a protest against the Chinese government's Tibetan policy. There she met a Parisian monk. "I paint beautiful pictures," she told him, "but there is so much to be done in the world that sometimes I feel like I need to do more than paint." "It doesn't matter what you do but how you do it," the monk responded. He meant well, but it did nothing to quench the fire in Liora's belly to be of service.

Ten years later, Liora, who is a bird-watcher, was looking for information about them. While online, she discovered the Elephant Listening Project,[2] a not-for-profit organization associated with the Bioacoustics Research Program (BRP) at The Cornell Lab of Ornithology, and signed up for information. From time to time they sent her emails but, until recently, none that addressed the poaching crisis. "I remember them stating in an email, 'They [the elephants] are more like us than you think,'" she shared. "That intrigued me, and I started to fall in love with them."

A Seed of Truth

"People say, How's it going? I say according to plan. I don't know whose plan but it's going according to someone's."

—DENNIS NADEAU, CEO Whiz Gaming, Inc.

One day Liora received an email from the Elephant Listening Project asking for donations. Her first thought was that she needed to invest in the protection of the elephants she loved. Her second thought was to contact them to ask permission to use their photos, and they agreed to partner with her. Now Liora also partners with The David Sheldrick Wildlife Trust.[3] In both cases, 50 percent of net proceeds from her elephant paintings are donated to these organizations.

Although one of her earlier pieces was shown in the White House and is now in the Smithsonian Institution, Liora knows for the first time in her career that she is living her purpose. "This is my destiny," she tells me with certainty. Sure, she could have picked any worthwhile cause and been of service, but they didn't spur her to action. It was only upon learning about the plight of the magnificent elephants that her purpose was revealed. Sometimes we reach our destiny in spite of ourselves.

DESTINY AND FREE WILL

Some readers will dismiss the idea of destiny. They think they alone determine the course of their lives. It's all about hard work, good decisions, and some lucky breaks or so they claim. Others believe that there is a plan and that there's not much any of us can do to alter it. You were dealt the good cards when you came into this life or you weren't. Perhaps, however, it is a combination of the two. What if there is a master plan for every life and we also have free will. This means that the plan is not written in stone and thus we can influence it depending on how we interpret and respond to the situations and people in our lives. Our energetic, emotional, physical, and behavioral response then magnetizes a particular variation of our future. In this way, we co-create our lives.

Of course, it may not feel that way when we are going through our day-to-day lives. Sometimes no matter what we do, our purpose and the lucky breaks we seek don't knock on our door. Remember that it took Liora twelve years until her purpose revealed itself. She's not unusual. Destiny has a timing of its own. Yet, when you review her story, two elements stand out. The first is that she had a strong intent to be of service in the world. That didn't go away even though she didn't know how to manifest it. The second is that without her conscious knowledge, she was taking steps that helped her reach her destiny. She just didn't see the progression or how things were connected. That seems to be how it works.

Some people beat themselves up when they don't see progress, thinking that in some way they are not good enough. This does nothing to change their lives for the better or accelerate their growth. All it does is deplete their confidence. In response to their inner fear, they may try working harder, which increases their stress level.

"When I try to make it happen, force it, and figure it out, I become frustrated," Patricia Varley, a small business owner, told me. She continued:

"I tend to want it immediately and if it doesn't happen right away, I become worried, fearful, and doubt myself. However, when I quiet my mind and just show up in life without an agenda, that's when what needs to happen next reveals itself. It takes patience, trust, and an intuitive knowing that things will get handled. The answers are coming, not from me trying to figure it out, but by priming the stage, stepping back, and letting it come to me.

"As a coach and leadership trainer, I've made my living by working with clients nationally and internationally. A couple of years ago, I fell in love with a man who lives in Hawaii. Now my dream is to work locally so I can be with him, expand my presence on the Internet, and take my knowledge base to the next level so I can guide my clients to a deeper level of change. Although I've tried everything I could think of, I haven't found any work in Hawaii. I also don't have the technical skills to expand my Internet presence nor do I have the money to hire someone. In addition, although I sense that there is a deeper level from which to do my work, I haven't found the right training opportunity. Until this week, that is.

"Three things occurred this past week that surprised me. First, people I know who have a sustainability company asked me to provide leadership training within their workshops on Oahu, the island that has the most business. This could lead to other opportunities with them as well as introduce me to new potential coaching clients.

"Second, although I didn't think it would serve my business at all, this week I gave a speech at a local dance event. I only agreed to present in order to spend some time in nature, see my friends, and dance a little. However, after delivering my hour and a half speech, which to my surprise was videotaped, the owner of the company that produced this event, which provides dance events all around the world, approached me with a business offer. He said I was a natural teacher and asked me to provide a series of classes that would be videotaped and placed on his website, which has thousands of followers. This would not only get my name out, I would also share in the profits his website generated.

"Last, I ran into a woman I know who teaches energy work in corporations. She invited me to attend without charge a workshop she is presenting in the next couple of weeks. I have the intuition that this is the upgrade in my work I've been seeking. After all the years of overthinking and trying to force my will, I realize now that sometimes there are things that I have no control over that have to happen before what I want can come to me."

A Seed of Truth

*"Slow down and everything you are chasing
will come around and find you."*
—AUTHOR UNKNOWN

What then do you do while you are waiting for your purpose to be shown, your dreams to manifest, and/or your destiny to be revealed? What follows is a four-step map.

1. Keep the Faith

When our greatest trials are upon us, when we don't know our direction and we question whether our abilities are enough, keeping the faith is the most powerful thing we can do. Faith is about affirming the future you desire. It is about strengthening and extending your energetic intention no matter what circumstances you encounter. Faith is about believing in yourself though you are imperfect and a work in progress. It is about remembering who you are at your deepest essence and not being sidetracked from that perspective. Faith often appears with her sister "hope," whose purpose is to keep your dream energized.

Most people play it small. They just want their problems to be solved and their day-to-day existence to be more comfortable. They want incremental change. Sure, they may say they want the big dream, but they stay on the receiving side of it rather than the creating side. They ask or even plead for what they want rather than affirming that they already have it. Yet, they don't extend their energetic intent or fishing line to that which they desire in order to hook it and live big. In other words, they don't expand their energetic size (not their ego) in order to accommodate the largeness of their dream.

Now, of course, you don't always get what you want. Thank heavens. If I had gotten every job, client, or lover I so desperately wanted, my life would be a mess. Wisdom is knowing that what comes to you is yours and what passes you by is meant to be, whether or not you understand the reasons.

2. Feel Where You Are

The second thing you need to do while waiting for your needs and/or dreams to be fulfilled is to maintain connection with your inner self. As discussed throughout the book, wherever you place your attention becomes your center. When you place your attention inside your mind/body instead of your thinking mind, emotions, sensations, and insights become available to you. These point the way to an inner map that enhances your balance, solidity, confidence, and spaciousness. Instead of resisting pressure and thus living in a contracted, small, and tense way, you are best positioned to attract what is yours to have and to embody when you feel where you are and allow pressure to expand you.

3. Reflect on the Choices You Make

So many of the everyday choices we make are not really choices; they are automated responses that are programmed in our minds. From time to time, we all need to step back and get some distance from how we function in order to see the bigger picture of our lives. Take a walk in nature. Watch the rain from your window. Reflect on who and where you are now in your life. View yourself with the love of a gentle mother or a wise grandfather. Ask yourself, what misunderstandings do you have about success that creates additional pressure? How much is enough to satisfy you? If you could say no to something in your life without creating any consequences, what would that be? Now look at that issue again to see if there are consequences, whether they matter, and if they do, how you can prevent or minimize them. Remember, each of us is not just a responder to what life brings; we are also creators.

Your current reality may not be comfortable or desirable; in fact, it may be downright painful. What is your ownership in this? So much of what stresses us is the small stuff. For example, Janice, an executive director of a nonprofit organization, came into my office so tense I could feel her rigidity. The public relations firm she hired had sent back copy filled with numerous grammatical mistakes. Instead of sending the piece back and telling them to fix it so she can focus on her dream of making her organization the go-to place to learn about creating community, Janice spent time editing their work and resents it. "Can you see your ownership in this?" I ask her. "You do have other options than to do the work yourself." Janice looks at me surprised. She hadn't even thought about that before she edited the piece.

Dan, the vice president of a pharmaceuticals company, dreams of becoming the successor to the current president. The boss is grooming him for the job, but instead of believing in his dream and his capabilities, he stresses when he has to make a decision. He's so afraid he'll make the wrong one that his self-doubt paralyzes him. His procrastination ripples through his organization, creating frustration and uncertainty among his staff. If he could just step back and look at the big picture, would he still choose to postpone and let fear and the need for perfection rule? Alternatively, would he be decisive and then, if necessary, realign just as pilots do? Sometimes "ready, fire, aim" is appropriate.

Each of the people in these examples is caught in a cycle that keeps them playing it small. When you are waiting for your dreams to manifest and for your destiny to show itself fully, don't wait to be pushed into greatness. Instead, connect to your inner core and then, in service of the greater good, LEAP!

4. FOLLOW THE CLUES

And so we return to where we began. Follow the clues that lead back to yourself so you meet life with a flexible strength, presence, and confidence. Follow the clues not just with your cognitive intelligence but also with your emotional and intuitive intelligence. Follow the clues through the drought and through the desert until they are raining all around you. Follow the clues knowing that the pressure you feel is the energy you need to do the job. Follow the clues knowing that some things, situations, people, or abilities may be taken away during the process but new ones—better ones—will appear.

For example, in 2009, my mother, Sally Bernstein, had a stroke that brought on the beginning of dementia. At first, when she would fall or not be able to do what she was once able to do, she would become angry. She wanted control of her life back. She was used to holding her head high and now felt ashamed that she had to use a walker and later a wheelchair. Over the next four years, her ability to stand, button her blouse, and, at times, express herself was taken from her. With every loss, she had to learn to accept her current reality. I'm sure her ego took a beating. Over time, she learned to accept what was with a grace that was truly inspiring. Although limited physically and mentally, my mother lived the last years of her life in a state of goodness, kindness, and love. It was a privilege to witness and be of service to her. As it was when I was young, she had become my teacher. My mother had come full circle and returned to her essence. When she died on December 20, 2013, she passed with a little smile on her face.

So now, you've heard my stories and learned the tips and practices, and how they can be applied in your workplace so that you and your team can thrive on pressure. If you've read with an open mind, something has already shifted in you. Can you feel your new power? Now that something has changed in you, how will your story be different? What commitments will you make and what steps will you take to reinforce this next best version of you? All of us teach what we have to learn. Now it's your story that needs to be told.

RESOURCES

EMBODIED LEADERSHIP WORKSHOP PROVIDERS/AIKIDO IN BUSINESS

United States

South Florida
Aimee Bernstein, Open Mind Adventures
(561) 734-8982, www.openmindadventures.com
aimee@openmindadventures.com

San Francisco Area
Robert Nadeau, City Aikido
1339 Mission St., San Francisco, CA 94103
(415) 552-7208, http://www.cityaikido.com/robert-nadeau-shihan
-aikikai-aikido

Richard Moon, extraordinarylistening.com
moonsensei@gmail.com

Richard Strozzi-Heckler, Ph.D.
Strozzi Institute
4101 Middle Two Rock Road
Petaluma, CA 94952
http://strozziinstitute.com/

Jamie Leno Zimron
LPGA Pro / The Golf Sensei
Aikido 5th Dan / Somatic Psychologist
Peak Performance Speaker-Trainer
www.thekiaiway.com
760-492-GOLF (4653)
jamiesensei@thekiaiway.com

Michigan
Paul Bohlman
aikidobloomfield@gmail.com
(248) 885-5737

New Jersey
Andrew Cohn
Lighthouse Consulting
W: 610-649-0892
M: 610-246-3367
Email: andrew@lighthouseteams.com

Washington
Christopher Thorsen, Radical Inquiry
QuantumEdge.org
ct@quantumedge.org
Office 360-331-1149 Cell 415-740-0727

England

Mark Walsh
Integration Training
mark@integrationtraining.co.uk
http://www.integrationtraining.co.uk/

Israel

Miles Kessler
Dharma Teacher, Aikido Sensei, Director of The Integral Dojo
"Changing The Way We See The World"
Office: +972-(0)3-562-4164
miles@theintegraldojo.com
www.theintegraldojo.com

NONPROFITS

Aikido Without Borders (AWB) is an NGO using aikido to teach young people on both sides of the conflict concrete and positive replacements for violence, hatred, and aggression. By bringing these young people together to have joint trainings in aikido and conflict resolution, AWB is creating new and lasting connections that lead towards a more peaceful future. Currently, they are working with Israeli and Palestinian youth; however, they plan to expand to other populations.

The Mastery Institute for the Public Benefit is an experiment in multi-sector collaboration, created by Aimee Bernstein and The Spirit of Giving Network in Boca Raton, Florida. Working with CEOs/executive directors of organizations that serve the public, the institute helps them expand their organizational and leadership impact. As part of this endeavor, mind/body/energy training is available to participants to help them skillfully handle the demands and pressure of their work.

Aiki Extensions is dedicated to applying and promoting the principles and methods of the nonviolent martial art of aikido in all aspects of life. We accomplish this through

- Action—Extending aiki principles and methods to novel training sites, problem situations, and areas of conflict.
- Collaboration—Supporting and enhancing communication among the world's largest community of aiki practitioners.
- Exploration—Pursuing and promoting deeper understanding of the application and effect of aiki principles in the world.

For more information visit www.aikiextensions.org.

ENNEAGRAM RESOURCES

Helen Palmer

- *The Enneagram: The Definitive Guide to the Ancient System for Understanding Yourself and the Others in Your Life,* Harper & Row, Publishers, San Francisco, 1988
- *The Enneagram in Love & Work: Understanding Your Intimate & Business Relationships,* HarperSanFrancisco, 1995

David Daniels, MD

- *The Essential Enneagram,* HarperSanFrancisco, 2000

Don Richard Riso and Russ Hudson

- *The Wisdom of the Enneagram,* Bantam Books, New York, 1999

Michael Goldberg

- *The Nine Ways of Working: How to Use the Enneagram to Discover Your Natural Strengths and Work More Effectively,* Marlowe and Company, New York, 1996

NOTES

CHAPTER 1 RUN DEEPER, NOT FASTER

1 Katie Hafner, "For Second Opinion, Consult a Computer?" *New York Times,* December 3, 2012, http://www.nytimes.com/2012/12/04/health/quest-to-eliminate-diagnostic-lapses.html?pagewanted=all&_r=0

2 Roland Fisher, *State-Bound Knowledge in Consciousness: Brain, States of Awareness, and Mysticism,* Daniel Goleman and Richard J Davidson, eds., Harper & Row, 1979, pp. 92–93.

3 http://www.theworldcafe.com/

CHAPTER 2 DON'T BELIEVE EVERYTHING YOU THINK

1 Adapted from Helen Palmer, *The Enneagram: Understanding Yourself and the Others in Your Life*, New York: HarperCollins, 1988.

2 I used this old saying recently and the person didn't get it; so to illustrate its meaning just in case you missed it, try pointing your second finger; your pinkie, ring, and middle fingers are pointing back at you.

CHAPTER 4 FUNCTION FROM YOUR CENTER

1 Elmer Greene and Alyce Greene, *Beyond Biofeedback,* Santa Barbara, CA: Knoll Publishing, 1989

2 Richard Strozzi-Heckler as quoted in "Centering and the Development of Leaders—Part I: Just Stop the Reaction!" *Cultivating Leadership,* posted

by Carolyn Coughlin, March 5, 2012, http://www.cultivatingleadership.co.nz/embodied-leadership/2012/03/centering-and-the-development-of-leaders-part-i-just-stop-the-reaction

3 Jim Loehr and Tony Schwartz, "The Making of a Corporate Athlete," *Harvard Business Review,* January 2001, p. 120.

4 World City, November 21, 2103, http://worldcityweb.com/event-coverage/hr-connections/437-work-life-balance-european-institute-for-social-capital-offers-company-certification

CHAPTER 5 WHEN THINGS ARE BAD, ENVISION YOUR BEST

1 Norman Doidge, MD, *The Brain That Changes Itself: Stories of Personal Triumph from the Frontiers of Brain Science*, New York: Penguin Books, 2007.

2 "Stroke Recovery Solutions with Dr. George Bach-y-Rita (caregiver of Pedro Bach-y-Rita)," http://www.strokerecoverysolutions.com/custom-1/StrokeRecoverySolutionswithDrBachyrita.pdf

3 William Bridges, Ph.D., *Surviving Corporate Transitions: Rational Management in a World of Mergers, Start-ups, Takeovers, Layoffs, Divestitures, Deregulation and New Technologies*, New York: Doubleday, 1988.

4 Ron Kurtz and Hector Prestera, MD, *The Body Reveals: An Illustrated Guide to the Psychology of the Body*, New York: Harper & Row/Quicksilver Publishers, 1976, p. 1.

5 Dana R. Carney, Amy J.C. Cuddy, and Andy J. Yap, "Power Posing: Brief Nonverbal Displays Affect Neuroendocrine Levels and Risk Tolerance," *Psychological Science,* 21, no.10 (2010) 1363–1368.

6 Mihaly Csikszentmihalyi, "The Flow Experience in Consciousness: Brain, States of Awareness and Mysticism" in Daniel Goleman and Richard J. Davidson, eds., *Consciousness: Brain, States of Awareness, and Mysticism,* New York: Harper & Row, 1979.

7 William F. Russell, *Second Wind: The Memoirs of an Opinionated Man*, New York: Random House, 1979.

CHAPTER 6 SIZE MATTERS

1 Based on David Daniels, MD, *The Essential Enneagram*, San Francisco: HarperSanFrancisco, 2000.

CHAPTER 7 GAIN CONTROL BY GIVING IT UP

1 Julia Boorstin, interviewer, "The Best Advice I Ever Got," *FORTUNE Magazine*, March 21, 2005, p. 103.

2 Thomas F. Crum, *The Magic of Conflict*, New York: Simon & Schuster, 1987, p. 25.

3 Ibid., p. 153.

4 Ibid., p. 105.

5 Arik Hesseldahl, "The Intel-AMD Settlement: A Play by Play," *Bloomberg BusinessWeek,* November 15, 2009.

6 "Advice" by Bill Holm in *The Chain Letter of the Soul: New and Selected Poems,* Minneapolis: Milkweed Editions. Copyright © 2009 by Bill Holm. Reprinted with permission from Milkweed Editions. "Advice" by Bill Holm in *The Chain Letter of the Soul: New and Selected Poems,* Minneapolis: Milkweed Editions. Copyright © 2009 by Bill Holm. Reprinted with permission from Milkweed Editions.

CHAPTER 8 NOBODY DOES IT ALONE

1 Hillary Rodham Clinton, *Living History*, New York: Simon & Schuster, 2003, pp. 161–162.

2 Dr. Joel & Michelle Levey, *Living in Balance*, Berkeley, CA: Conari Press, 1998, pp. 114–115.

3 "Item 10: I Have a Best Friend at Work," *Gallup Business Journal*, May 26, 1999, http://businessjournal.gallup.com/content/511/item-10-best-friend-work.aspx

4 Lyubomirsky, S., L. King, and E. Diener, "The benefits of frequent positive affects: does happiness lead to success? *Psychological Bulletin,* 131(6), 2005, pp. 803–855.

5 Joel H. Head, ACC, and Joshua Freedman, "Inspiring Employee Engagement through Emotional Intelligence," *Six Seconds*, January 2, 2014, http://www.6seconds.org/2014/01/02/employee-engagement-emotional-intelligence/

6 http://charterforcompassion.org/

7 http://compassionateaction.org/

8 "Louisville Becomes International Compassionate City," November 11, 2011, http://charterforcompassion.org/city-campaigns

9 Ibid.

10 Paul Marsden, "Memetics and Social Contagion: Two Sides of the Same

Coin?" *Journal of Memetics—Evolutionary Models of Information Transmission,* 2, 1998, http://cfpm.org/jom-emit/1998/vol2/marsden_p.html

11 Jonathan Haidt, "Wired to be Inspired," *Greater Good; The Science of a Meaningful Life*, March 1, 2005, http://greatergood.berkeley.edu/article/item/wired_to_be_inspired

12 "Billion Dollar Man Richard Branson's Advice For Entrepreneurs," December 13, 2013, https://www.youtube.com/watch?v=_xKRWVBlP3U

13 Jonathan Haidt, *The Happiness Hypothesis: Finding Modern Truth in Ancient Wisdom*, New York: Basic Books, 2006, pp. 28–29.

CHAPTER 9 SPARK CREATIVE SOLUTIONS
IN HIGH-PRESSURE SITUATIONS

1 Seth S. Horowitz, "The Science and Art of Listening," *The New York Times Sunday Review*/The Opinion Page, November 9, 2012.

2 Paul McCartney, Classic Vinyl Radio interview, February 11, 2014.

3 Alden M. Hayashi, "When to Trust Your Gut," *Harvard Business Review*, February 2001.

4 Tom Davenport, "Big Data and the Role of Intuition," *Harvard Business Review*/HBR Blog Network, December 24, 2013, http://blogs.hbr.org/2013/12/big-data-and-the-role-of-intuition/

5 Dale Evans, "The Workplace of the Future," *Huff Post Impact*, August 12, 2013, http://www.huffingtonpost.com/dave-evans/cisco-the-workplace-of-future_b_3744016.html

6 Gen. Charles C. Krulak, "Cultivating Intuitive Decisionmaking," *Marine Corps Gazette*, May 1999, http://www.au.af.mil/au/awc/awcgate/usmc/cultivating_intuitive_d-m.htm

CONCLUSION: YOU REACH YOUR DESTINY
IN SPITE OF YOURSELF

1 To see Liora Davis's art go to http://lioraart.com

2 The Elephant Listening Project, http://www.birds.cornell.edu/brp/elephant/index.html

3 The David Sheldrick Wildlife Trust, http://www.sheldrickwildlifetrust.org/index.asp

INDEX

action
    through energy concentration, 97
    in flow state, 109
    and integrity, 76
    intent of, 21
    as personality-informed, 45
    skillful, 21–22, 110, 120
"Advice" (Holm), 157
aikido
    in business retreats, 84
    conflict resolution in, 149, 150–157
    essence of, 7
    to handle pressure, 16
    training in, 3, 6, 20
    unbendable arm practice, 112
alpha state, 196
amygdala, 151
anger triggers, 124–126
appreciation exercise, 178
Arnst, Tim, 73
arrogance
    and energy level, 103
    and fear of inadequacy, 132
    habitual, 66
    of leadership, 131
    and presence, 105
The Artist's Way (Cameron), 71
attention
    and emotional expression, 173
    focus of, 4–5, 56–57, 61–67, 221
    future-directed, 59, 63, 88
    influences on, 57–58
    in listening, 192

    in meditation, 208
    on mind/body, 20
    open, 67–70
    and perceptual centers, 78
    refocus exercises, 60, 71–72
    shifting, 129
authenticity, 76, 82, 165, 207
autonomic activity, 16
awareness
    and centering, 81
    in flow state, 109
    focused, 56
    and mastering pressure, 18, 20, 22

Bach-y-Rita, George, 95–96
Bach-y-Rita, Paul, 95–96
Bach-y-Rita, Pedro, 95–96, 97, 111
balance
    of perceptual centers, 79
    under pressure, 77
    in working life, 86, 92–93
Barrett, Scott, 10–11, 86
Bass, Mark, 197
behavior
    changing, 20, 49, 78, 177
    and personal development stage, 148
    workplace patterns of, 135–136
beliefs
    conflicting, 107
    limitations of, 159
    vs. preferences, 49
Bernstein, Sally, 223
Beyoncé, 1–2, 120

Beyond Biofeedback (Green), 77
Block, Peter, 212
body
    awareness of, 18, 88–89, 90
    feedback from, 72, 77
    hereness of, 18–21
    in meditation, 209–210
    mind interaction with, 77–78
    and outer-directed attention, 63
    perceptual centers of, 78–79
    reactions to pressure, 11
The Body Reveals (Kurtz and Prestera), 105
Boss personality type (Type 8), 42–43, 47, 48,
    50, 125, 126, 146, 148
brain
    and arousal level, 16
    conflict reaction in, 151
    cortisol effect on, 12
    in stroke recovery, 96
    worldview imprinted in, 32
brain waves, 195–196
Branson, Richard, 177
breathing
    in centering practice, 80, 88, 90
    in conflict resolution, 152
    from *hara*, 79
    importance of, 148
    in meditation, 208–210
    personal practice for, 25–26
    and refocusing attention, 60
    to shift state of mind, 133
    for team meetings, 213
Bridges, William, 102
Brown, Juanita, 28, 29
business
    conflict resolution in, 152–153
    and positive emotions, 165–167
    presence as power in, 104
    shared ownership in, 212
    and worldview, 32, 38, 43, 51
business strategy, 72–74, 84–85

Cameron, Julia, 71
Cellular One, 16, 84–85, 136
centering
    and attention influencers, 58
    and balance, 77
    business application of, 84–85, 94
    in conflict resolution, 152
    and control, 147
    experience of, 79–84
    and *hara,* 79
    and integrity, 76
    and *ki,* 102
    in meditation, 209, 210
    and pace of activity, 59, 65
    practice exercises, 87–89, 90–92
    under pressure, 85–87
    and problem solving, 206–207
Citigroup, 142
Citrix, 161–162
Clinton, Hillary Rodham, 163
cognitive reframing, 123–124, 129
Cohn, Andrew, 147, 151
collaboration
    and conflict resolution, 157–158, 161–162
    and worldview, 49, 52
collective unconscious, 191
compassion
    benefits of, 172
    in conflict resolution, 155, 159
    and gender, 174
    as happiest state, 165
    and heart energy, 186
    and judgmentalism, 49
    and meditation, 208
    and open attention, 69
    and personality type, 35
Compassionate City Campaign (Louisville,
    KY), 169–171
competitiveness, 36, 38, 164
conflict
    avoiding, 42
    of beliefs, 107
    defined, 139
    identifying issues in, 139–141, 159–161
    point of view in, 148–149
    reacting to, 82, 141–148
    resolving, 7, 150–157
    workplace, 138, 161–162
confluence, 154
control
    in conflict resolution process, 154
    gaining by relinquishing, 138, 142–148, 182
    when listening, 192
coping strategies, by personality type, 45–47
cortisol, 12, 105
counter-phobic personalities, 40, 46
Covey, Stephen, 66
Creative Visualization (Gawain), 106

creativity
    and brain wave frequency, 196
    and intuition, 201
    and meditation, 208
    and pressure, 191
criticism
    and personality type, 34, 39, 124, 143, 144
    reacting to, 97, 176–177
Crum, Thomas, 142, 149
Csikszentmihalyi, Mihaly, 109

Daffner, Richard, 195
The David Sheldrick Wildlife Trust, 217
Davis, Liora, 215–217, 218
decision making
    and attention focus, 59, 63
    and centering, 81, 82
    inclusive, 166
    and integrity, 76, 93
    intuitive, 197
    and meditation, 208
    and personality type, 38, 42–45
    procrastination in, 222
    and worldview, 49, 52
deep breathing, 25–26, 133
deep relaxation, 16
destiny, 107–108, 217–218, 220–222
Detwiler, Jim, 80
diet, and stress, 15
disease
    and meditation, 208
    stress-related, 77, 164
Dixon, Jim, 16–17, 18, 84, 136
dreams, 191, 202–206
Drucker, Peter, 89

ego
    and conflict resolution, 141, 157–158
    and expanded feeling, 103
    and skillful action, 21
    and version of self, 124, 130–131
Einstein, Albert, 184, 193
Eisner, Michael, 194
Elephant Listening Project, 216–217
emotional burnout, 181
emotional intelligence, 166, 167, 182
Emotional Intelligence (Goleman), 151
emotions
    vs. cognitive mind, 78
    conflict-triggered, 151, 159

    detachment from, 81–82
    expressing, 172–174
    and intuition, 194
    positive influence of, 172
    in workplace, 164–169, 172, 179–188
empathy
    and gender, 174
    and heart energy, 186
    in hostage situation, 138
    and outer-focused attention, 61
employee recognition, 114, 165, 177, 178
energy
    defined, 2
    emotional effect on, 172
    flow of, 13–14, 97, 107, 108–111
    fluctuations in, 85–86
    and *hara,* 79
    to/from heart, 176, 178, 185–186
    increasing, 22, 81
    intent/direction of, 100–101, 220
    interactions with, 2–3
    interference with, 142
    mastering, 89
    in meditation, 209
    movement of, 102–103
    and open attention, 69
    and personal qualities, 103–104
    power/intensity of, 101–102
    in quantum physics, 12
    relinquishing, 58, 159
    self-centered, 65
    for task completion, 15
Energy Age, 12
Enneagram
    function of, 6–7, 32–33
    origin of, 32
    personality types in, 33–45
    stress/anger triggers in, 124–126
    using, 52
entitlement, sense of, 66, 132
Epicure personality type (Type 7), 41–42, 47,
    48, 50, 125, 146, 148
exercise, benefits of, 15, 133
extraordinarylistening.com, 149, 191

feedback
    from body, 72, 77
    in workplace, 176–177, 178
First Union National Bank (Broward County,
    FL), 167–168

Fischer, Greg, 169
flow state, 108–111
free will, 217–218
Friedman, Howard, 164
Fumasoni, Marcelo, 93
future
    as attention focus, 59, 63, 88
    belief in, 96, 111, 220
    destiny vs. free will, 217–218

Gawain, Shakti, 106
Ginsberg, Yvonne, 176, 183
Giver personality type (Type 2), 34–35, 46, 48,
    50, 124, 141, 143, 147
Goleman, Daniel, 151
Google, 176, 183–184, 194
gratitude exercise, 114
Green, Alyce, 77
Green, Elmer, 77
grounding
    and balance, 77
    business application of, 94
    in conflict resolution, 152
    and *ki*, 102
    and outer-focused attention, 63
    practice of, 89, 133–134
    and problem solving, 206–207
GTE, 84

habit(s)
    appreciation as, 177–178
    of attention, 57, 61
    changing, 49
    energetic, 3
    identifying, 18
    imprinting, 106
    as mode of action, 45
    self-centered, 66
Haidt, Jonathan, 172, 177
happiness, 165
hara, 78, 79, 88, 208–210
head, as perceptual center, 78–79
heart
    energy to/from, 176, 178, 185–186
    as perceptual center, 78
    and power, 101
HeartMath, 172
heart rate, 13, 172
hereness, 18–21, 22, 58, 65

Heschel, Abraham J., 141
Hill, Michael Brandon, 137–138, 148
Holm, Bill, 157
hormones
    and power projection, 105
    and pressure reactions, 12
Hudson, Ross, 52
Huizenga, Wayne, 11–12, 14
humor
    in centering practice, 88
    and state of mind, 133

Ichazo, Oscar, 32
Idea Champions, 196
immune system, 12, 164
inner-directed attention, 65–67, 71
inner map, 6, 7, 22, 97, 110, 209, 221
integrity
    in business, 83
    and centering, 81, 82
    defined, 76
    losing, 77
    mind/body, 80
    and outer-focused attention, 61
    and power, 101
    work/life, 92–94
intuition
    availability of, 191, 193
    awareness of, 77
    vs. cognitive mind, 78, 193, 194
    function of, 193–195
    power of, 18, 20, 190
    stimulating, 195–202
Isaacs, David, 28, 29

Jobs, Steve, 56, 72
Johnson, A.G. (Buddy), 167
Jordan, James, 148
judgmentalism, overcoming, 47–50, 148
Jung, Carl, 191

ki, 6, 97, 101, 102, 104, 105, 110,
    112–113
kindness communities, 182–183
knowledge
    in intuition, 195
    as power, 39, 161
Krulak, Charles C., 197
Kurtz, Ron, 105

Lakhiani, Vishen, 113, 114, 115
leadership
  blending points of view in, 149
  and ego, 130–131
  embodying, 2, 18, 21
  emotional support to/from, 175–176,
    186–188
  employee perceptions of, 166–167
  and intuition, 194
  and mastering pressure, 17–23
  and organizational focus, 73
  and power, 101
  presence of, 17, 105, 106
  worldview of, 52
leadership mastery formula, 22
Lennon, John, 193
Levey, Joel, 164
Levey, Michelle, 164
life
  balance in, 86, 92–93
  breath as essential to, 148
  destiny in, 107–108, 217–218,
    220–222
  as energetic system, 100–101, 103
  flow of, 109–110
  modern, 59, 88
listening
  and centering, 80
  in conflict resolution, 149, 154, 155
  vs. hearing, 191–192
  and open attention, 69
  to our bodies, 11, 20
  to our minds, 32
  in problem solving, 198
  in workplace, 211–213
Living History (Clinton), 163
Living in Balance (Levey), 164
loneliness, 66, 78
Louisville, KY, 169–171

The Magic of Conflict (Crum), 142
Mandela, Nelson, 191
Marsden, Paul, 171
Marshall, Marjorie, 4–5
McCartney, Paul, 193
McKiernan, Michael, 161, 162
mediation process, 140, 152–153, 158
Mediator personality type (Type 9), 43–45,
    47, 48, 50, 126, 147, 148

meditation
  benefits of, 208
  brain wave frequency during, 196
  at companies, 213
  deep relaxation in, 16
  group, 115
  hara in, 79
  practice exercise, 208–210
  to shift state of mind, 133
  as stress reducer, 15
memory, 16, 208
mind
  body interaction with, 77–78
  cognitive, 20, 78, 79, 108, 109, 151, 193, 194,
    199
  deceptions of, 32
  reactions to pressure, 11
  state of, 119–120, 129, 133
  subconscious, 194, 195, 196
mind/body/energy system
  awareness of, 77–78
  energy spirals in, 102
  energy streaming through, 6, 15, 97
  and flow state, 109
  ideal state of, 2
  intent in, 21
  personal practice for, 7
  pressure exerted on, 14, 191
  reframing in, 129–130
  size changes in, 118
  and visualization, 106
Mindvalley, 113–116
Moon, Richard, 56, 84, 136, 149, 191, 206
movement
  of energy, 102–103
  to open attention, 72
  to recenter, 86–87
multitasking, 59

Nadeau, Robert, 3–4, 6, 20, 101, 108, 119–121
narcissism, 66
negativity
  and conflict resolution, 140, 141, 178
  countering, 98–99, 129, 177
  and lower self, 119
neural pathways
  and aikido techniques, 6, 17
  and flow state, 110
  imprinting through practice, 20

neural pathways *(continued)*
    and *ki,* 105–106
    and personality type, 33
    and shifting state of mind, 133
    and stress reduction methods, 16
Novartis, 93–94

Observer personality type (Type 5), 38–40, 46,
    48, 50, 125, 140, 146, 147–148
open attention, 67–70
organizational culture
    and behavior patterns, 136
    changing, 171, 172–184
    emotional support in, 164, 166, 167
    employee identity within, 211
    focus on critical in, 72–74
    and leadership, 52, 131
    and team personalities, 52–53
outer-directed attention, 61–64, 72
overthinking, 41, 78

Palmer, Helen, 33
Parsons, Richard, 141–142
perceptual centers, 78–79
Perfectionist personality type (Type 1), 33–34,
    45, 47, 48, 50, 124, 143, 147, 180
performance
    and attention, 56
    and awareness, 20–21
    and pressure, 13, 14, 108
    and visualization, 106
    workplace, 166
    and worldview, 49
Performer personality type (Type 3), 36–37,
    46, 48, 49, 125, 144, 147, 180
personality
    breaking free of, 45–50, 78
    and conflict resolution, 140–141
    and control, 147–148
    mental patterns in, 32
    and stress/anger triggers, 124–126
    in technology industry, 161
    type, 33–45 *(see also* Enneagram)
    in workplaces, 51–53
    and worldview, 42–47
Personal Practice
    assessing pressure management approach,
        24–26
    centering, 90–92
    developing *ki,* 112–113

function of, 7
giving/receiving heartfelt energy,
    185–186
influence of worldview in, 51
meditating, 208–210
refocusing attention, 71–72
resolving conflict, 159–161
shifting version of self, 133–135
phobic personalities, 40, 46
Piazza, Antonio (Tony), 139–140, 152–153,
    158
point of view
    in conflict resolution, 148–150, 152, 154,
        155–156
    when listening, 192
posture, 72, 90, 105
power
    and breathing, 25
    vs. force, 101
    through knowledge accumulation, 39,
        161
    and posture, 105
    presence as, 104–106
    relinquishing, 58, 62, 96
practice. *See also* Personal Practice
    of centering, 80, 87–89, 90–92
    for flow state, 110
    to imprint new behavior, 20
    in using intuition, 197–198
presence
    and attention focus, 62, 68, 69
    and centering, 81
    and *ki* flow, 97
    of leaders, 17
    power of, 104–106, 120
    respect transmitted by, 121
pressure
    in aikido practice, 6
    and breathing, 25
    centering to handle, 85–87
    defined, 13–15
    and leadership, 17–18
    learning to use, 2–5, 15–17, 108, 158
    and level of consciousness, 120
    in modern life, 59
    in motivating change, 23, 191
    and personality type, 143–147
    reactions to, 11–12, 32, 85
    resisting, 96
    and skillful action, 22

Prestera, Hector, 105
problem solving
    centering in, 206–207
    dreams in, 202–206
    intuition in, 194–202
    listening in, 192
    meditation in, 210
productivity
    in caring workplace, 167
    and friendship, 115, 165, 166
    monitoring, 162
    and positive energy, 113
    and stress reduction, 15
    U.S., 166
profit sharing, 114

relationships
    and attention focus, 59
    and cognitive mind vs. heart, 78
    and dropped attention, 66
relaxation
    and attention, 56
    breathing technique for, 25–26
    deep, 16
Ricard, Matthieu, 165
Riso, Don Richard, 52
Romantic personality type (Type 4), 37–38, 46,
    48, 50, 125, 144, 147
Ross, Steve, 142
Russell, Bill, 109

Samuels, Stephen, 132, 197–198, 199
Second Wind (Russell), 109
seizures, 4
self
    appreciation of, 178
    connecting to, 71–72, 221
    listening to, 192, 199
    multiple versions of, 119–128
    shadow side of, 135–136
    shifting versions of, 129–135, 157–158
self-awareness, 20, 39
self-centering, 65–66
self-confidence
    and attention focus, 62
    and centering, 81
    and presence, 105
self-doubt, 40, 41, 82, 164, 222
self-esteem, 61
serotonin, 12

skillful action
    and level of consciousness, 120
    and mastering pressure, 21–22
    practice for, 110
sleep disturbances, 11
spiral movement, 102
states of consciousness
    accessing, 16–17
    and brain wave frequency, 195–196
    and dreams, 202
    and presence, 105, 120
    for relaxation, 15
    shifting, 56, 119–135
    and stress/anger triggers, 126
Stewardship (Block), 212
stress
    from beta brain waves, 196
    disease related to, 77
    dissipating, 158, 172
    and emotions, 164, 172
    and energy flow, 15, 97
    keeping perspective on, 221–222
    and lack of focus, 57
    and negativity, 99
    and personality type, 143–147
    triggers of, 124–126
    and workplace friendships, 165
stress reduction
    assessing effects of, 24–25
    conventional approaches to, 15–16, 78
    and inner map, 110
    and meditation, 208
    new approaches to, 16–17
    showing appreciation as, 178
    and worldview, 50
Strozzi-Heckler, Richard, 21, 79
Strozzi Institute, 21
success drive, 36–37, 49
sweating, 13, 16

talking stick, 212–213
Tan, Chade-Meng, 183
team applications
    assessing performance under pressure,
        26–29
    focusing on critical issues, 72–74
    function of, 7
    identifying team worldview, 51–53
    increasing positive energy, 113–116
    integrating work/life, 92–94

team applications *(continued)*
    resolving conflict and collaborating, 161–162
    shifting versions of self, 135–136
    spreading kindness, 186–188
    supporting intuition, 211–213
technology
    dominance of, 10
    as industry, 161
telepathic communication, 12
testosterone, 105
theta state, 196
Thorsen, Chris, 84, 136
Thrun, Sebastian, 194
Time Warner, 142
Trooper personality type (Type 6), 40–41, 46,
    48, 50, 125, 146, 148
Tuff, Antoinette, 137–138, 148

values
    being grounded in, 82
    comparing actions to, 18
    corporate, 166, 167
Varley, Patricia, 218–219
visualization, 97, 106–108, 112–113, 115, 196
vulnerability, 179–180

well-being
    effect of stress on, 164–165
    features essential to, 32
    and focus of attention, 56, 61
    and heart energy, 186
wisdom
    enhancing, 120
    group, 94, 212

    and open attention, 69
    and wish fulfillment, 221
The Wisdom of the Enneagram (Riso and
    Hudson), 52
work. *See also* organizational culture; team
    applications
    balance in, 86, 92–93
    collaboration at, 157–158
    conflict at, 138–141, 161–162
    emotional support at, 164–169, 172,
        175–176, 179–188
    feedback at, 176–177, 178
    friendships at, 115, 165
    and integrity, 76
    listening at, 192, 211–213
    satisfaction with, 10, 173
    shifting state of mind at, 133, 135–136
    stress reducing techniques at, 5
World Café, 28–29, 94
The World Café (Brown and Isaacs), 29
worldview
    and business view, 51
    and emotional expression, 173
    in Enneagram, 33
    function of, 32
    overcoming judgmentalism from,
        47–49
    and personality type, 34–47
    of teams, 51–53

Yes . . . AND? Technique, 98–99, 112

Zappos, 211
the zone, 15, 108

ABOUT THE AUTHOR

Aimee Bernstein is a change accelerator, licensed psychotherapist, and president of Open Mind Adventures, which specializes in leadership and personal development. For over thirty years, she has coached and consulted Fortune 500 executives, entrepreneurs, scientists, and professionals in high-pressure environments, helping them refine their leadership vision, skills, and presence, and manage organizational change. Her work, which draws from psychology, organizational development, aikido, and meditation, teaches how to use pressure—the energy of change—to develop mastery over oneself. She focuses on building emotionally intelligent, collaborative teams and work cultures, resolving conflict harmoniously, and sparking the creative solutions and innovations that make a positive difference. Aimee's clients have included The Ritz-Carlton Hotel Company, Dolce & Gabbana, The Port of Singapore Authority, and Microsoft Latin America.

Aimee received her graduate degree from Boston University in counseling psychology and interned at Massachusetts General Hospital under the auspices of Harvard Medical School. She is a skilled facilitator and an internationally acclaimed speaker. In 2014 she cofounded The Mastery Institute for the Public Benefit in Palm Beach, Florida, to enhance the impact of 501(c) organizations. She is listed in *Who's Who in American Women* and is the author of numerous articles and stories.

Aimee is a former rock and roll and light jazz singer who now performs in the shower. She is a devotee of salsa dancing and laughter.